THE
MASTER KEY TO CHINA

THE
MASTER KEY TO CHINA

DAVID CLIVE PRICE

The Master Key To China

First published in 2014 by
Panoma Press
48 St Vincent Drive, St Albans, Herts, AL1 5SJ, UK
info@panomapress.com
www.panomapress.com

Book layout by Charlotte Mouncey
Printed on acid-free paper from managed forests.

ISBN 978-1-909623-50-7

To Simon

For his infinite patience and support

ACKNOWLEDGEMENTS

I WOULD LIKE TO THANK the people who have helped in the process of researching and preparing this book, as well as those people whose consistent support and advice have brought it to final fruition. In particular I would like to express my gratitude for the encouragement of my fellow members of the Pacific Basin Economic Council, Chairman Wilfred Wong and Chief Executive Deborah Biber, as well as Dr. Frank-Jürgen Richter of the annual Horasis Global China Business Meeting, where I shared many discussions with Chinese and global CEOS about the future of the Chinese economy and its unique market characteristics.

I would also like to express my gratitude to the experts: Walter Jennings, Managing Partner Greater China of Kreab & Gavin Anderson Hong Kong, Hugh Purser and Jonathan Mantle of the Republik of Kreative Ekonomie, Dr Robin Pharoah of Esro Limited, Jeff Tucker of March Publishing Cambridge and Alan Barrell, Entrepreneur in Residence at the Judge Business School, Cambridge University for their insights on China and permission to use the Map of China image on page 62. Finally, I would like to thank my excellent editor Stephanie Lawyer, the indefatigable Mandy Gibbins-Klein and Emma Herbert of Panoma Press, my inspirational mentor Rachel Henke, Lisa Cafiero of Write the First Time, and Simon Chu whose consistent support and patience enabled me to see this book through to completion.

PRAISE

Inspiring, motivational and generous

I really enjoyed this book. In addition to being a good read that imparts a lot of important information lightly, The Master Key to Asia *made me think more deeply about the countries in Asia I have visited and done business, and the ones I haven't and want to. For a small book it packs an enormous punch! It's inspiring, motivational and generous in its advice. I could have gone on reading twice as long. I shall recommend it to anyone and everyone going to Asia whatever their purpose.*

Jonathan Mantle, bestselling author of *Companies That Changed the World* and co-founder of Republik of Kreative Ekonomi

Savvy and concise from an Asian master

The Master Key to Asia *is the right book at the right time about the right areas of the world for many businesses and business people.*

There has been so much nonsense written about doing business in Asia that it is refreshing to come across a short how-to guide that touches on the most important aspects of managing relationships, cultural pitfalls and expectation management. David correctly gives the theory and cultural relativism a miss preferring to concentrate on what actually happens at the coalface. And he should know. Having spent most of his career

*advising senior Asian CEOs, pitching for business in
Asia, writing about Asian businesses and running
his own consultancy from Hong Kong, Taiwan and
the Philippines, he is eminently placed to provide this
useful primer. Concise, savvy and very helpful. I will
recommend it to my clients.*

Mark Dailey, Strategic Communications Consultant,
Madano Partnership UK

Guide to feeling comfortable and confident in Asia
*Drawing from a wealth of experience in Asia, David
Clive Price has written an easy to navigate book that
guides business people or entrepreneurs though the
complex maze of Asian cultures. Offering valuable
information on business practices, social behaviours,
ethics, and religion, this book delves deeper into Asian
cultures and helps you understand the 'why' so you
can feel comfortable and confident interacting with
others as quickly as possible. It is a must for any
international business professional. It's great also
for students who want 'real' information about Asian
cultures. I highly recommend this book.*

Kara Ronin, Director Executive Impressions, US and
France

How not to be a barbarian at the gates
*David Clive Price really knows his Asia. He has toured,
lived and worked in just about every corner of it,
so he speaks from a wealth of personal experience.*

Better than that, he possesses the talents of a skilled negotiator and mediator. There can be no better guide to preparing the newcomer to this culturally rich and diverse region for the task of dealing with Asians on a business level. And preparation is the key to this process, for the novice has first to know who and what he is up against, and what to expect of the encounter. The Master Key to Asia *is essential reading for those about to knock on Asia's door — if they are to avoid being seen as barbarians at the gates.*

Peter Moss OBE, Director of Government Information Services, Hong Kong (retired)

THE business travel guide for Asia

David Price has, through his long and enlightened journey across Asia, acquired an impressive amount of anecdotes, experiences, knowledge, wisdom and 'cultural insider information' which he generously and frankly shares (to the extent of sometimes sharing with us personal details) in this reference book. Being myself a Japan business expert, I do fully agree with the author's advices and tips, and I do personally think that, especially in Japan and Asia, business and culture are widely connected.

Starting by explaining the basics/fundamentals of Asian Business Culture (patience, long-term relationships, face saving, family ownership, trust building), David Clive Price then refines his analysis by delivering an outstanding country-by-country overview, which makes this book really UNIQUE. Indeed, there are many books out there covering specific topics about specific countries of Asia (I am the author of one of them), but a well-written and well-thought guide to a dozen of Asian countries is a rare TREAT! That is why I recommend this masterpiece, this 'Bible of Asian Cross-cultural Communication', without reserve.

Philippe Huysveld, Director Global Business and Management Consulting, France

A great resource for intercultural organisational communication tactics

As a student at Rowan University studying communication studies, I've taken a vast interest in intercultural communication. This book provides great detail on how to communicate in intercultural business settings. I was surprised at how much information this book holds!

Keith Du Barry, Graduate student, New Jersey, US

West meets East

I found this book really helpful for looking at the cultures of East and West from both ends of the spectrum, especially in relation to business. The format is clear, and the author's tone is inspiring and helpful. There are also some intriguing stories and humorous comments to make the lessons easily digestible. There's no doubt there's a need for books like this, especially with so many different Asia cultures to consider. In fact, I would have liked a bit more on each country (China, Japan, Malaysia, etc.), but since this is first in the series, I guess that's in the pipeline. Overall, I would say buy this book if you want to develop business in Asia and build up your Asia skills.

Simon Dowell, Business Development Manager, UK and Hong Kong

Master key master
This book is a great guide to learning how business is conducted in Asia, and how each of the region's cultures and markets are subtly but significantly different. It's full of the author's deep knowledge of Asia culture and business, has action points that make the lessons learned easy to implement, and provides a clear and innovative system for taking your business in Asia to a whole new level. I'd certainly recommend it to newcomers and to those already there.

Douglas George, Producer 'The Money Programme', TVB Pearl Hong Kong

AUTHOR'S NOTE

As a special thank you for purchasing this book, please enjoy my free bonus gift 'Chinese Communication and Culture Cheat Sheet', which is available at my companion website http://davidcliveprice.com/the-master-key-to-china-book-gift/. You can also find a wealth of other information and resources on the site.

I hope the following will be of great value to you. Please be kind and review this book on Amazon.

Other Books on Asia by David Clive Price

- *The Master Key to Asia,* Amazon Paperback and Kindle 2013

- *Moonlight Over Korea*, Amazon Paperback and Kindle 2012

- *The Scent of India* by Pier Paolo Pasolini, translated by David Clive Price, Amazon Paperback and Kindle 2012

- *Buddhism: The Fabric of Life in Asia*, Formasia Books 2008

- *Within the Forbidden City*, Formasia Books 2004

- *Neon City Hong Kong*, Cameraman 2002

- *The Food of Korea*, Periplus Editions 2002

- *Travels in Japan*, Olive Press 1987

For a full-sized, full-colour version of the books with description, and to order copies, simply go to http://www.davidcliveprice.com/master-key-asia and http://www.davidcliveprice.com/books-articles

China has a massive trade surplus,
but a vast cultural deficit with the world.

Hu Jintao, former president of China

PREFACE

THE MASTER KEY TO CHINA aims to offer an essential business guide to Chinese economic life and the diverse regions in which it is based. Understanding China better through enhanced cultural awareness is the key to business success and to the professional development and personal confidence that drives that success.

Performance is largely results driven in the West. Many business people wanting to launch in China wonder why they should learn a lot of 'touchy feely' stuff about culture and history and traditions. In their eyes, they are up to speed on operations and nuts-and-bolts issues. What else is there? They think it's better to arrive, make some deals and worry about the finer points later.

They are wrong. Competitive intelligence goes beyond the basic business issues and deal-making to the very core of what makes for long-term business success. Without a basic understanding of how Chinese business culture works, or any willingness to learn, companies often make mistakes that can set back or destroy their business plans altogether. It would be far better to invest in market knowledge and cultural understanding at the outset.

This book is intended for those companies, SMEs and entrepreneurs that want to invest time and resources in China for the long run. Not only those who are preparing to enter the markets there, but those who are already there and developing their platform, those who are headquartered or based in more 'Western' and cosmopolitan cities like Hong Kong and Singapore and plan to expand further into China, and those in core Europe, Britain, America, Canada, Australia and New Zealand that see China and its diverse economies and cultures as the key to future success in the global economy.

CONTENTS

INTRODUCTION

WELCOME AND THANK YOU for choosing to read this book. I hope you will find it a wise investment, for it is an investment both in yourself and in the future of your business.

As the centre of the world's economic gravity moves towards the East, there could not be a better time for unlocking and developing new markets or a more urgent need to rise to the challenge of growth, innovation and personal development that these emerging markets present. In the midst of economic uncertainty in the West, more and more people are looking for new opportunities and strategies that lie beyond their familiar horizons.

Why is China so important?

No other region on earth has caught the attention of global businesses so much as rapidly expanding China. This vast country is poised to become the world's leading economy. Although its annual GDP growth rate has slowed from the 9.5 per cent average the country achieved in the decades since 1995, GDP growth of around 7.5 per cent is still the envy of many countries in the world. GDP per capita in China is around US$6,100 as compared to US$50,000 in the US and US$46,000 in Japan. However, China has vowed to quadruple this by 2020 on the back of an economy rebalanced towards consumption and services rather than manufacturing and exports. Despite a litany of ills including corruption and pollution, the productivity of one-fifth of mankind is now being unleashed.

Some simple facts bear this out. China is producing more than seven million university graduates a year. By 2020, it will have 195 million graduates, more than the entire workforce of the US. China is already the leading filer of patents and trademarks in the world and will soon surpass the US in scientific citations.

The country is witnessing the growth of rapid transport links such as an extensive high-speed rail network, and planned global transport links across the Asian countries to the Middle East, Russia and Europe. In 1983, it took three days to travel by train from Guangzhou to Beijing. Now it takes eight hours. Five of the world's top eight container ports are in China. Through a multiplicity of regional free trade areas and agreements in and across Asia Pacific, China is set to become a global mega-trader through an unrivalled system of global connectivity.

China's middle class is growing at the rate of a hundred million every few years. By 2020 almost a half of China's population will be middle class. In tandem with this, China is witnessing the largest urbanisation drive the world has ever seen as people migrate from the country to the cities. It is estimated that 221 new cities each with a population of over one million will be added by 2025, compared with only thirty-five such cities in Europe at present. There will be ten mega-cities in the inner provinces, each with a population of some sixty million (roughly the size of the UK). This will vastly increase the number of China's consumers.

Now more than ever there is a need for companies outside China, or those fortunate enough to already have a foothold there, to develop their presence, pursue opportunities and create long-term relationships with their potential Chinese partners, suppliers, customers and investors.

As Francis Fukayama declared in *Trust, the Social Virtues and the Creation of Prosperity*, Free Press 1996, 'economic life is embedded in social life, and it cannot be understood apart from the customs, morals, and habits of the society in which it occurs. In short, it cannot be divorced from culture.' Nowhere is this truer than in China. Understanding the culture of China, which includes the business practices, business etiquettes, social and familial behaviours, approach to ethics, cultural traditions and spiritual beliefs of the country as a whole as well as of individual provinces and cities, is vital to business success.

The Master Key to China is written specially for those entrepreneurs and companies both large and small that want to quickly find their feet or develop their footprint in this fascinating and complex country, home to potentially the largest but also the most diverse consumer class on earth. The easy-to-follow chapters provide a logical roadmap so that you can find your way in a complex and difficult business culture that may seem daunting at first. However, China offers increasing rewards to those who stick to the path and accept the need to learn new rules and approaches.

China is by no means a homogenous country. However, there are customs and attitudes that are common to almost all regions that lie within and beyond the Great Wall and are bounded to the east by the East China Sea, to the north by Mongolia and Russia, to the west by Kazakhstan, and to the south by Vietnam, Laos and Myanmar. These customs and cultures mark China out as unique.

Doing business in China is different from doing business anywhere else in the world, largely because of the special emphasis placed on indirect and intangible values such as building credibility, relationships and trust rather than on immediate business returns and bottom lines. That said, there are also fascinating and subtle differences in the way individual Chinese companies approach these intangibles based on their respective cultural beliefs, level of affluence and exposure to international trade. This inevitably results in some marked differences in management attitudes from province to province.

For example, top management in Beijing or Shanghai may understand their business world very differently to their counterparts in Xining or Chengdu, and all of them may have different expectations of a partner from Western countries. At the same time, each member of the business community across China cherishes certain cultural and social beliefs that they expect the foreign partner to make some attempt to grasp.

The master key to doing business in China is to gain an adequate understanding not only of the country's business assumptions and culture as a whole but also those of the individual cities and provinces that make up China's colourful patchwork quilt. By *understanding* I mean more than doing research. I mean acknowledging that you have your own cultural style and approach, which are rooted in your education and upbringing. The ingrained assumption that there is only one (largely Western) way of doing things is very difficult to shake off.

But unless you are ready to recognise the differences between your personal and professional style and that of the business community of the market in which you are aiming to succeed, you will never fully unlock the potential of China.

Building new business in China's dynamic and diversified economy is an enormous challenge. It requires confidence. It requires the courage to learn new viewpoints while re-assessing your own. It requires the flexibility to change and accept change. It requires a willingness to develop new aspects of yourself and your business as well as a sense of other perspectives.

In other words, if you want to learn the secrets of success that lie within China's vast economy, you have to discover how to turn the master key in the lock and push the door open. That master key is culture, and business culture above all.

Who should read this book

There are four main groups of people who will benefit from reading this book:

- Firstly, companies large and small, business owners and entrepreneurs planning entry or developing their business in one or more markets in China. They will need a clear plan of action for understanding essential cross-cultural differences between Western countries and China, applying general principles and lessons learned to specific business operations such as working, meeting, communicating, relationship building, networking and negotiating with clients, partners and colleagues from different cities and provinces in China.

- Secondly, business leaders who want to develop their intercultural leadership skills and exhibit appropriate behaviour to project confidence, commitment, sincerity, positivity, sensitivity and wisdom across cultures, as well as genuine interest in and passion for the culture and beliefs of their host country. This includes developing presentational skills, ability to deliver inspiring and motivational speeches, hosting dinners and events, and being a guest at banquets.

- Thirdly, CEOs and senior executives who manage cross-cultural teams of expatriates and locals that operate in China, building their confidence to recognise and handle cross-cultural issues in the workplace as well as to provide them with the skills to build strong work relationships, create trust and build respect and credibility in the Chinese business world.

- And fourthly, all those who regard the discovery of new cultures as being an essential journey for expanding their own horizons, improving their ability to interact with and understand other people and their beliefs, and who never want to stop learning or developing themselves. Respecting other cultures provides food for the soul and stimulation for the mind. Crucially, it breeds confidence and confidence breeds success.

CHAPTER ONE

GETTING READY FOR CHINA

ONE OF THE MOST SIGNIFICANT elements in China's national psyche is pride in a cultural history that stretches back almost four thousand years and that makes China the world's most ancient, uninterrupted civilisation. For the Western business person going into China (or already there), it is sometimes easy to forget that the modern technocratic face of the Chinese political, business and educated élites masks a strong sense of continuity with traditions, beliefs and customs that stretch way back in time.

It is not easy for the Western executive to get a hold of the rolling, complex and epic proportions of Chinese history, but it is certainly worthwhile to get some sense of the unfolding tale because of the perspectives it throws on modern Chinese attitudes and behaviour.

Origins of Chinese culture and cultural attitudes

Despite appearances to the contrary in China's burgeoning cities and mega-cities, China has always been a rural society built on farming communities. A journey of perhaps less than an hour from some urban conglomeration can lead the traveller directly to a landscape and way of life that seems hundreds, if not thousands of years old. These often impoverished communities have survived through time, cataclysmic changes of government and natural disasters, by banding together as cooperatives in which obedience to the group is far more important than individual initiative or independent thinking. Even with growing urbanisation leading seven hundred million people to the cities in the near future, and government policies that have lifted four hundred million Chinese out of poverty in the last twenty years, a communal and rural mind-set still exists among the majority of city dwellers.

This mind-set extends to the inherited tendency, still discernible among the general population, to regard commerce and business as necessary evils that are less dependable than farming, which in the past was the real producer of China's wealth.

Historically, merchants were held in lower esteem than farmers, while the 'foreigners' who tended their flocks in pastoral communities beyond the agrarian inner provinces were held in even lower regard. Since this was their only experience with foreigners, the Han Chinese tended to consider all foreigners as culturally inferior. It is worthwhile to remember that, from the time of its unification some two thousand years ago, the Chinese name for China has been two characters that mean 'Middle Kingdom'.

Another enormous influence on Chinese culture was the teachings of the philosopher Confucius, who lived around the fifth century BC. It is no surprise that the emperors of China, ever since the founding of the

Forbidden City in Beijing in 1420, worshipped at the Temple of Agriculture, the altars of the Earth, Sun and Moon, and the shrine to Confucius. This moralist and social visionary taught that society was pyramid shaped, deriving from the emperor at the apex, with scholars, officials, farmers, artisans and merchants below. Each class was expected to respect and give loyalty to those above them, and the entire system was given validity by the incorruptibility and quasi-divine nature of the emperor at the top.

The family system was regarded as a microcosm of imperial society as a whole. The most important element of this system, which still has a place in the Chinese mind-set and behaviour of today, is that respect and deference are given to superiors. Just as the pyramid structure, rank and status still play an important part in Chinese values, even if these values are being subtly challenged by the younger generation, so too does a very strong emphasis on respect or giving face. In this paternal society, women are expected to defer to men, the eldest male is the head of the family, younger brothers are to defer to elder brothers, younger sisters to elder sisters and so on.

In fact, Confucius built a strong system of family values and teamwork on the basis of the existing collectivist rural society. It is noticeable that many private Chinese businesses, not only in Mainland China but also in Hong Kong, Singapore, Taiwan and Malaysia, are family companies with a paternalistic head of the family, a network of inter-family responsibilities and obligations, and a succession policy often based on the next male successor in line.

Another continuing cultural influence on modern Chinese society is Taoism, which derives from the writings of Lao Tzu, a philosophical contemporary of Confucius. Whereas Confucius wrote about the place of humans in society, Lao Tzu wrote about the connection of humans with nature. The concept of the opposing but complementary forces of Yin and Yang that drive the universe comes from Taoism. The infinite shades of grey implied by the mingling of feminine and masculine, black and white, passive and active, create a middle ground or 'the Way' between extremes. As such, Taoism can still be seen as active in Chinese sensibilities when Western executives try to enforce strict rules about quality control or even contracts. The infinite shades of Taoist grey may well be the reason why the apoplectic Westerner cannot understand the Chinese counterpart's refusal to accept contracts as binding or final, even after they are signed.

Following Confucianism and Taoism, the next largest belief system in China is Buddhism. Buddhists believe that only after living through various cycles of reincarnation, in the form of different living beings, all the sorrows and misdeeds of life will disappear. First introduced into China by monks from India and Nepal in the first century AD, Buddhism spread throughout China and competed with Taoism. Buddhism became the primary belief system in China from around 600 AD to the tenth century, when the emperor sponsored Confucianism in response to the threat of Buddhist dominance. This dominance was dealt a much more severe blow during the Cultural Revolution, when worship was prohibited and many temples were destroyed. However, with the growing sophistication and cultural hunger of China's aspiring middle classes, Zen Buddhism is making a marked comeback in the country.

Finally, China's history has been plagued by foreign invasions. The Huns, the Mongols, the Manchu have all terrorised or enforced degrading rules, such as the wearing of pigtails, on the indigenous Han Chinese population. The Opium Wars between 1839 and 1860, initiated by British gunboat attacks on China's coastal towns to enforce the import of opium, and the subsequent Taiping Rebellion, led by a Chinese zealot who believed he was the son of Christ, caused untold death and suffering — and hatred of all things foreign. The invasions continued, with the Western powers enforcing economic zones of influence on China; the Japanese annexing Chinese territory in 1895 and indulging in the Nanking Massacre of 1937; the Americans and Russians backing opposing sides in the Civil War between the Kuomintang Nationalists and the Communists; and the subsequent flight of the Nationalists to Taiwan to set up their own government under the protection of America.

This is just a snapshot of five hundred years of Chinese history to give you an idea of why modern China has been suspicious of foreigners, or at least wary of them. It also explains why the notion of victimhood, recovery of national pride, and rejection of any suggestion of Western condescension has played such an important role in the Chinese renaissance and China's rapid progress to being, once more, one of the world's leading economies as it was in the early nineteenth century.

However, these ingrained reactions, although deep in the Chinese national psyche, are not necessarily shared by the vast numbers of China's educated élite and middle classes, who are increasingly cosmopolitan, often educated at the very best schools and universities abroad, speak good English, are technologically sophisticated and well travelled. Although it is true that many modern Chinese in the country may well stare at foreigners as a rare and exotic breed, seeing them as some kind of celebrity, the vast majority in cities now regard foreigners as part of their increasingly globalised way of life. Indeed, a foreigner in a provincial city, although seen as slightly odd, may also be regarded as a sign of approaching wealth and economic success.

Chinese business environment

There is no doubt that the mixture of Confucian, Taoist and Buddhist influences on the way Chinese think about life and do business is less visible to the unsuspecting Westerner than it was twenty years, or even ten years ago. There is a surface veneer of intense modernity and cosmopolitanism to the residents of the first-tier cities (Beijing, Shanghai, Guangzhou, etc.) and big coastal cities of China that would seem to imply that amid all the advertising hoardings, the large cars, the latest mobile phones and electronic gadgets, the speaking of English, the sparkling skyscrapers, and all the other signposts of a thriving 'Westernised' society, the Chinese way of doing business is becoming more or less similar to that in Western countries.

However, scratch beneath the surface and many foreign executives will find that the Chinese business environment, although apparently Westernised, retains many of the traditional characteristics of Chinese culture. Family values remain extremely important, as Confucianism dictates, with high respect for seniority and the elderly, and those children who are not sent off to college or university in the West remain in the family home until they are married. However, there is one exception to the Confucian rule that emphasises the predominance of the male line, which is still observed in Japanese and Korean families and business. In China, communism's emphasis on everyone being equal means that there are many more women in business, and in positions of power, than in other Confucian societies.

Due to their history, the Chinese are polite but often slow to accept any outsider into their charmed family circle or local network. To the foreigner, they may seem to be not very trusting and even secretive or 'unreadable'. But even within their own circles, the Chinese can be very slow to accept others. If you speak the same dialect or come from the same village or locality, it is much easier to be accepted. What is true at the local level is even truer at the big-city level, where identity and trust are preserved through behaviour that may seem clannish to the outsider. This closed mentality means that foreigners must devote time and effort to getting into the circle of trust by slowly building good relationships.

Generally speaking, in Chinese business the question of the deal (the 'offer'), the potential profits, the possible transaction, the organisation you represent, even the win-win benefits of a proposal will be considered as secondary to the question of whether your Chinese counterpart will feel comfortable doing business with you. In other words, trust (*xinyong*) has to be established. However, trust usually takes a considerable time and a lot of entertainment and socialising. Chinese business is above all personal, and it is as a likeable and well-respected person that you will succeed, not necessarily as a professional as in the West. That is why first impressions are so important in Chinese business etiquette and in all Chinese business negotiations. Senior Western executives should make sure that they fulfil the expectations of Chinese protocol when they meet their Chinese counterparts and that junior managers do the same. The Chinese will expect similar ranks to be matched with similar ranks in meetings, and that their Western counterparts build a personal relationship with their equals in the pecking order. Companies that rotate their staff in their China offices, or their senior executives, will often find that the relationships have to be formed all over again.

Business relationships in China are generically called *guanxi*. I will discuss guanxi in Chapter Five, but for now suffice it to say that guanxi is a form of networking or mutual obligation that creates a circle of trust. You cannot survive in business in China without guanxi, whether it's at the highest government level or in a small town in Xinjiang province. The essential element is that one member of the circle of trust helps another overcome difficulty at some point, and that this favour is reciprocated at a later date. In many ways, the Chinese form of guanxi has influenced or is related to the way business is done all over Asia. Instead of targeting a key decision-maker as in the West, users of the guanxi network go 'round to work' (to use Polonius's phrase in Hamlet). They use members of the network to put pressure on the decision-maker through their personal relationship. This creates debts of obligation that can be called in at a future date.

Probably the most basic aspect of doing regular business with the Chinese, and also the most enigmatic and complex, is the need to give, save and not lose face (*mianzi*). Although you may find avoiding embarrassment, or a reluctance to make unnecessary enemies, is usual in some Western companies, saving face in China is a Golden Rule. There are all kinds of ways in which this applies, and which the unwitting Westerner may well consider too trivial to be of importance or be too wrapped up in their own way of doing things to notice how it impacts on others. Making awkward comments about the food at a banquet may cause unpardonable loss of face, insisting on a reply to an unanswered email or proposal may mean loss of face to you or (worse) to your counterpart, paying the bill at a dinner when you are not the host, and a million other sensitive situations are possible danger zones for face and should be negotiated with great care.

On the other hand, giving face is highly recommended, and this can be achieved through such simple means as complimenting a city for its modernity, admiring some local cultural exhibit or architecture, and by making concessions before, during and often after negotiations. If you adopt a tough, take-it-or-leave-it approach in China, you are unlikely to succeed. The individual, aggressive approach may work in Western business circles but in China everything is focused on team performance, and group decision-making, which often means that the decisions are worked out through slow-moving and complicated bureaucratic hierarchies.

This makes it even more important not to lose your cool. In fact, if there is one recommendation I would make above all others in Chinese business culture it is to cultivate patience. China is a vast and complex market that has attracted companies and entrepreneurs from all over the world with the promise of huge and untapped markets. Some of these companies have found success, but many more have not — and one of the principle reasons for not being successful has been their lack of patience. This and the complexity, variety and sheer rapid evolution of China's many markets (it is by no means a homogenous one) have caused countless mistakes and failed strategies and collapsed partnerships.

However, Western companies should take heart from the experience of Japanese and South Korean and Taiwanese businesses, which have had similar difficulties in tapping China's markets despite having a much closer understanding of China. Much of the reason for this is that China under the earlier decades of communism developed in a different way to Japan or South Korea or Taiwan. If you look at the map of China's provinces and the map comparing provincial economies with other nations' GDP (page 62), you will see that China's extreme geographical, social and cultural differences are similar to those of a huge federal entity like the European Union. Individual provinces are as culturally and economically different as Romania is from Sweden.

If you add to this diversity thousand of years of history and culture, and the extreme rapidity of China's rise towards becoming the world's largest economy, you have the ingredients for a unique and constantly developing business culture. Elements of this culture are changing all the time under the impact of globalisation, the internet, growing consumer sophistication and above all the education of Chinese in the West and their ability to travel and invest globally.

However, the essential conservative elements of face will likely remain constant in China, as will the need for building guanxi. If you have some appreciation of these cultural traits and practise patience, show professionalism and remain committed, the eternal process that is the norm for business in China may well speed up. Indeed, if you show some interest in Chinese culture and respect for Chinese business etiquette, you will make a positive first impression and be regarded as an educated and culturally knowledgeable person, which is of primary importance in a society that places such emphasis on education.

No book can fully prepare you for the niceties of Chinese business etiquette and for the inevitable mistakes that you are bound to make. Nevertheless, you can take comfort from the clear advantage you have as a foreigner. No one will expect you to be perfectly aware of Chinese etiquette, and your simple mistakes will often be indulged with humour. The important thing is to show that you are making some effort to understand and to fit in. This social indulgence may even give you some leeway in business negotiations, where you can use your ignorance of the office or guanxi system to be more direct than the Chinese themselves. Some Chinese business people appreciate Westerners getting to the point, if this directness is not taken to the extent of upsetting their co-workers and network. Don't forget that in a job interview in China, there's really only one question: Are you one of us — are you a part of the team? And if you're part of the team, welcome; we can always work things out. For many Chinese, the job interview lasts their entire career.

Finally, if you avoid making critical comments about China's politics or business practices, or showing your frustration, you will find that many Chinese have an innate respect for Westerners and for Western civilisation. Foreigners can still be considered a bit of celebrity in less developed areas and a Western business associate or friend can be a reason for inviting other Chinese round to admire this slightly exotic specimen, which only adds status to the Chinese host and confidence in you.

Action points

1. Write down six cultural or historical factors that may have influenced the way Chinese think about and relate to foreigners. Do you think any of these traits and influences are visible in your dealings with modern Chinese?

2. List out any ways in which Chinese you have met might seem clannish or protective of their own network and any examples you can think of when you felt excluded or not yet a member of the inner circle apart from not speaking Chinese.

3. Name three aspects of face that you consider slightly different to the usual Western instinct to save other people embarrassment. How do these express themselves as different?

4. Consider working with an experienced China executive coach or a local partner for the specific market or markets that you are targeting.

5. Get yourself informed about cultural differences by talking to local business people in China. Expatriate 'old hands' are also worth consulting. The combination of preparatory coaching BEFORE you launch your business and local advice makes all the difference to whether you connect or not.

CHAPTER TWO

THE CONFIDENCE FACTOR

When i first came to Asia, I didn't have much business experience and, above all, I didn't know much about the region except what I had read in novels and travel books.

And yet the country I chose was possibly one of the most culturally challenging in Asia: Japan. Very little English was spoken in Japan outside Tokyo (and often inside Tokyo) at that time, and although I found the country's complex traditions often fascinating, as a foreigner with only a superficial acquaintance with Japanese ways I was at best tolerated. Of course I made friends, I made contacts, I tried out some business ideas. I could just about cover the rent. But the curious thing was that the more I learned about the country and its culture, the more I spoke some basic Japanese, the less I seemed to make any progress. There was something missing.

It was only when I moved on to Hong Kong after a year in a love-hate relationship with Japan that I realised what that something missing was. Confidence.

Hong Kong at that time was a Chinese city but with British characteristics. Although I hated myself for thinking it, that British element was enough to get me into the Chinese world to such an extent that I ended up marrying a local Chinese and becoming part of a very extended Chinese family. As a result, I got to know all kinds of Chinese traditions and ways (for example, you don't take an apple from the pyramid of apples at the table for ancestor worship!), and the more I was accepted because I knew how to behave the more my confidence rose. I had a family around me, a promise of long-term relationships and support, and I had a strong incentive to become more ambitious.

Confidence, local knowledge and long-term intentions are essential to building a successful business in China. That is a central message of this book. They take time to show results, but those results are well worth waiting for.

It took me another few years in Hong Kong, dotted with successes and failures, for me to learn this. I was stubborn. I was still hooked on the dream of writing books more than taking a salaried job in a company and supporting my spouse and myself. I still didn't have the courage to take the leap into the professional world.

It was only when I was almost down and out that it occurred to me that I had skills that could be taken to another level. I had studied the history of ideas at university. I had a PhD. I could write. I could speak come Cantonese, even Mandarin. I had published two or three travel books about Asia, including a book on the Forbidden City and China's emperors.

The problem was that I was not applying any of this knowledge and competence systematically. I was not digging deep enough to develop my talents. I was not using my cultural confidence in any meaningful or consistent way. *Wake up and smell the coffee!* I told myself.

The chapters of this book are aimed at rectifying this lack of system and real confidence. They aim to create and sustain entrepreneurial flair. They end with 'Action points' that will help you build your business development plans for China as a whole, and for a number of individual Chinese markets in particular, so that you can move ahead with patience but also with the requisite confidence.

It took me a while to build a reliable brand and reputation for my business. That was probably because I lacked the kind of long-term vision that this book encourages. It is easy to go into China's markets with an ad hoc approach: a JV partner here, a local supplier there, an expatriate referral, a government agency, a local representative, a subsidiary, an online affiliate, and many other such combinations. You may even think that you can do it more or less from your home city by videoconferencing backed up with a occasional visit, or by winging it with a bit of help from a local Chinese and an expatriate or two.

But there is no substitute for entering China's diverse markets with *personal understanding* and experience of the cultural attitudes and business practices that are prevalent, rather than simply relying on market or product research, suppliers and distributors and local partners.

Eventually I ended up as the speechwriter for a major multinational bank, writing speeches for the chairman and CEO to give all over Asia and indeed all over the world as part of the preparations for Hong Kong's reversion to Chinese sovereignty in 1997. By the following year I had set up my own company, writing speeches and presentations for business and trade leaders, first in Hong Kong and then in other parts of China.

But it took me a long time to crack these other Chinese markets. They had cultural and business practices that were different to those of Hong Kong. I had to learn other Chinese business cultures and ways of doing things. Even though my previous work at the multinational bank had taken me to various provinces and cities of China, I was still an unknown in their eyes. I hadn't built the required long-term relationships or trust.

Every region and market in China is a challenge. That is another essential message of this book. Do not think you can automatically apply the knowledge gained about Chinese business culture as a whole to each and every province and city. If you have the skills and focus, if you have done the groundwork, if you have built the confidence through cultural understanding, you will probably be successful in more than one market. But to do that, you must also achieve mastery in more than one business culture.

So before we go any further, let's review what we mean by business culture. Because if you don't know what business culture is, and why it's so important, you will never be able to find the master key, let alone open the door.

Why is culture important in international business?

The cultural subtleties that influence international business reach far beyond the ability to greet your

Chinese counterpart correctly or choose an appropriate gift for a particular situation or present your business card in the right way.

The question of an individual culture's attitude to time and punctuality, whether the society is more collectivist in behaviour than individualist, the nuances of respect and hierarchy, not to mention body language and gestures and attitudes to harmony, can radically affect your understanding of the guy waiting in the next office or the woman across the dinner table, as well as your own chances of *being correctly understood.*

In a world of globalised business, the ubiquity of the internet and social media are no guarantee of avoiding unnecessary blunders (even insults!), while ignorance of who you are really dealing with may actively destroy your chances of building personal knowledge and creating the kind of credibility and trust that engenders long-term relationships and business success.

Even the way you frame your emails can jeopardise professional relationships across cultures. English may be on the way to becoming a lingua franca in some circles of Beijing or Shanghai, but in many parts of China there is a strong attachment to local languages, customs, dialects and deep-rooted beliefs. Ignore them at your peril!

The key elements of Chinese culture and business

As I said, I have spent more than half my life working as a speechwriter and 'strategic messenger' for major multinationals and government institutions in the East, and the other half in the West. I have also written several books and given speeches and talks on Asian culture and business.

The knowledge I have gained has left me in no doubt that Asian culture can be influenced by economic activity and globalisation. Anyone who has witnessed the rapid modernisation of South Korea or the impact of the markets on China in the last two decades will know that economics can indeed make a significant difference to cultural behaviour. However, this Westernising effect should not be exaggerated.

Unlike Western culture, which has changed and evolved over time, Chinese culture has always been much more traditional, introspective and fixed in the past. The accepted way of behaving in both social and business situations reaches back to traditions that are long established in Chinese history. One of the reasons why Chinese may find it hard to adapt to the Western way of doing things is that they take great pride in their culture, which provides them with models of behaviour that are often at odds with the way things are done in the West.

Correct etiquette

Like many countries in Asia, China is a complex hierarchical society (or number of societies) that has inherited numerous customs and rules that aim to show politeness and respect to superiors and elders. Social and workplace etiquette in China includes forms of address, where you must sit, to whom you can talk and in what manner. Many would say that this respect system is breaking down under globalisation and the different cultural demands and expectations of the younger Generation Y, but it is still largely true that decisions in modern China are made by the older generation, those who grew up either during the Cultural Revolution or during the rise of communist China. If modern Chinese ignore proper etiquette and protocols they will find it hard to develop lasting business relationships or gain promotion.

Filial piety

Respect for proper etiquette is related to filial piety, or how you interact with senior family members. The tradition of ancestor worship derives from ancient China, and even today memorials to dead ancestors are still displayed in family homes and temples. Obedience and respect are automatically given to the eldest member of the household. The decisions on where to go to school, what to study, what career to pursue, who to marry and even when to begin a family are still made by Chinese parents for their children. Even though there are an increasing number of exceptions, many young people follow the lifestyle and career chosen by their parents. Those who don't conform face unremitting pressure and critique to do so, both from their parents and from their social circle or community.

Tact and respect

The deference to family wishes is accompanied by respect for the feelings of friends, family and colleagues when, for example, a request is made. Instead of giving a direct yes-no response, most Chinese will find an acceptable, indirect way of conveying their response that doesn't upset the petitioner. They will buy time with a 'perhaps' or some other evasion so that they don't actually have to say no, and they will leave it to the other party to interpret their long silences or unanswered emails or letters. This is of particular relevance to Western executives seeking a straightforward reply, because they will not know that this is the normal behaviour expected of a cultured person.

Showing modesty

Modesty and keeping a low profile are qualities much admired by Chinese people. In everyday conversation, it is traditional for the Chinese not to boast about their achievements and status but to draw attention to those of others. In a similar way, the average Chinese will not try to stand out or give themselves a platform when compared to others. This attitude extends to the workplace, where an employee will draw attention to the contribution of the company and co-workers rather than beat his own drum. Those who draw attention to their performance are usually regarded as badly educated and arrogant.

Knowledge and education

Education and achieving degrees or certifications have enormous cachet in modern China. It was the custom in imperial China for those who aspired to higher social status and power to take the imperial civil service or scholar examinations. Passing these examinations conferred great local prestige on the successful examinee and opened up a career path in the Chinese administration, or even entry to the leadership élite. In modern China, Master degrees and PhDs from prestigious institutions, including many of the most respected universities overseas, are highly prized and respected by employers.

When Westerners first arrive in China, they may find these key elements of traditional Chinese culture alien or confusing when compared to the business environment in which they have grown up. Much more emphasis is still placed on the importance of family and relationships, of collective 'harmony and authoritarian decision-making, rather than on individualism and the more frank and open discussion that marks Western culture and decision-making. Nevertheless, for Western businesses and entrepreneurs working in China, it is vital to recognise the strengths of Chinese culture that may not be so evident in their home countries. Once harnessed, these strengths can become positive assets in a company's business dealings and human resources departments.

For example, despite the evasiveness of your Chinese counterpart, you can obtain an answer to an important question by changing the way you phrase the question or meeting with your customer in private. It may well be that modesty and indirectness of Chinese business people prevents them from rapidly getting to the point, but simple patience and a commitment to developing strong relationships can easily result in a positive outcome.

The point to remember is that all business in China is personal, so the longer the Westerner is in China and exercises patience, commitment and respect, the easier it will become to understand the thinking or intentions of a Chinese counterpart. China-based partners, employees, consultants and expatriates can also help in the process of correctly reading Chinese body language and facial expressions. In addition, immersing yourself in Chinese culture will gain you the respect of Chinese business partners and give you an insight into the Chinese mind-set. This in turn will help you gain the necessary face to build strong relationships and demonstrate correct behaviour.

To assist you in thinking about differences between Chinese and Western business attitudes, I reproduce below an excellent, if inevitably schematic comparison between Chinese and Western thinking and behaviour from 'The Chinese Negotiation' by John L. Graham and N. Mark Lam, *Harvard Business Review*, October 2003.

	Chinese	**Westerners**

Way of thinking

	Chinese	**Westerners**
Subject	holistic	individualistic
Social status	hierarchical	egalitarian
Relationship	beyond business	business networking
Logic	interrelated	sequential

Approach	authoritarian	open to discussion
Means	enforcement of order	fact-oriented
Channels	relationship	information
Duration	long-term	short- or medium-term

Business behaviour

Etiquette	formal	mostly informal
Meeting format	multiple objectives	clear objectives
Delegation	limited	authorised
Responsible party	normally unchanged	frequently changed
Information exchange	need-to-know basis	open exchange
Business proposal	arrived at indirectly	direct and open
Negotiation style	passive but persistent	direct and less patient
Priority setting	favourable total deal	principles and objectives
Expected partnership	long-term	business-driven

Action points

1. Study the chart above and then put a ruler over each column in turn, both Chinese and Western, to see if you can remember the difference in approach to each topic. You can practise this until you are more or less perfect. Thinking about the differences and what they might mean in real business terms will become second nature.

2. List out six cultural influences that you think are likely to make a difference in the way that the Chinese in general do business. Then map out the ways those influences (or some of them) may have an impact on the market or markets where you are operating or intend to operate.

3. Jot down the five basic elements of Chinese business culture with a short note on why they are so important and how you can follow them.

4. What do you consider to be the main strengths of Chinese business culture? How can you tap into these values in the specific market or markets that you are targeting?

To make matters easier for you, I've designed a **'Chinese Communication and Culture Cheat Sheet'**. All you need to do to access this special bonus is to join my mailing list by following this link: http://davidcliveprice.com/the-master-key-to-china-book-gift/

CHAPTER THREE

UNDERSTANDING THE CHINESE MARKET

CHINA IS THE MOST POPULOUS COUNTRY in the world with approximately 1.3 billion people. Han Chinese constitute around 92 per cent of the population with the rest being made up of more than fifty-five minority groups. It is important to remember that even within the Han Chinese there are significant differences in language and dialects, social customs, physical features and attitudes.

Diversity and demographics

The extraordinary rise of China has been well documented. The list of economic achievements over barely three decades continues to dwarf those of any other country in the world. With compound GDP growth of 9 per cent since 1995, China is already the second largest economy in the world and will soon be number one. It's already one of the world's top ten trading nations, the most popular destination for foreign direct investment, the largest mobile phone market, the largest auto market, the second largest personal computer market, the third largest advertising market.

China has cash reserves of some US$3.75 trillion. Nearly four hundred of the Fortune 500 companies have invested in China. Increasing urbanisation will see almost half the 1.3 billion inhabitants living in cities in the near future, and by 2020 it is estimated that ten new mega-cities will emerge in the inner provinces with populations reaching the sixty million mark, or the size of a country like the UK. It is no wonder that China is considered a great 'opportunity market' for Western goods.

But what actually is this market? Contrary to what many aspiring Western companies and entrepreneurs believe, China is still largely a developing country and consists of multiple markets segmented by regional economic development and local culture. Despite sharing a common language and many centuries of common history you should be aware that this vast country, in size similar to the USA or Europe, has a high level of diversity. There is a saying 'one China, four worlds', which refers to the wealth gaps between the highly developed mega-cities largely in the coastal areas, the moderately wealthy provincial cities, the less affluent country-level cities and the poor countryside.

Following the 'open door' policy announced by Deng Xiaopeng in 1978, coastal areas of China were the first to attract outside investment and have benefited the most from economic reforms. The vast interior provinces are lagging behind in economic development. Furthermore, the Chinese also have diverse cultural patterns exhibited by variations in dialects, values, lifestyles, traditions and customs.

For Western companies seeking entry and expansion in China, it is important to recognise that

China is actually a conglomeration of markets divided by such factors as level of economic development, industrial priorities and local cultures. In fact, its diverse mix of consumers, all with varying levels of purchasing power, means that China's provinces should be treated almost as a collection of separate countries. By 2020, economists predict that these separate provinces will consist of a loose union of second-tier developing and first-tier developed 'countries' with comparable GDPs.

The first map below shows the actual provinces of China, while the second map shows the GDPs of China's provinces by 2020 compared to those of various countries in the world.

China's Provinces

China's Provinces - Prediction for 2020 -
Provinces GDP's will equal many nations

China GDP in 2020 by province (projected): A Union of
Second-Tier Developed + Top-Tier Developing Countries

- Above $1,000bn
- Between $500bn - $1,000bn
- Between $100bn - $500bn
- Below $100bn

by permission
University of Cambridge
Source: HSBC, CEIC, IMF, CIA

As you can see, the comparison is quite startling. The
second map reveals dramatic differences between
provinces, but the most obvious factor is that the richest
provinces are all on the eastern and southern side of the
country. This reflects the location of China's largest and
most dynamic cities.

There is no formal definition of what constitutes
a 'first-tier', 'second-tier' or 'third-tier' city in China.
But it's commonly agreed that the top tier incorporates
Shanghai and Beijing, as well as Guangzhou and

Shenzhen, prosperous cities just across the border from Hong Kong and at the heart of the industrial Pearl River Delta. Not only are these cities in effect mega-cities with populations of some twenty million people but they also have the highest incomes in the country. However, they account for only 9 per cent of the country's population.

There are many more people living in the second-tier cities, often defined as the provincial capitals and special administrative cities — twenty-three in all. Although Shanghai and Beijing tend to be the cities that everyone talks about, many experts believe that the future of the country lies in its smaller cities. They are its heartland and the likely source of its most rapid growth over the next decade. More than three hundred million people live in China's smaller cities, roughly equal to the population of the US. Many Western companies are hoping to target the customer base and labour pool of these cities and slowly shift their focus from the developed eastern seaboard into the centre and west of the country.

All prefecture level or county-level capitals are generally classed in the third tier. But the difference between second tier and third tier is not very precise. Some experts set the barrier for a second-tier city at a population of three million and a minimum per-capita GDP of US$2,000 or more. Using that definition, there are some sixty cities that are second tier. In addition, China has 160 third-tier cities with populations of one million or more, out of about 655 cities in all.

However they are defined, it's clear that the importance of second- and third-tier cities is growing. Just as people are migrating from the countryside to the city in massive numbers, companies are migrating from the expensive coast to target the interior.

Another important cultural difference to consider is that between the older generation and what is called Generation Y, also known at the Millennials or the Post-1980s or the Little Emperors. This generation has grown up with the internet, mobile communication and social media as a natural part of their lives. They are probably the most important group for Western companies to understand today as their buying power is growing rapidly and they are also shopping on behalf of family members. They use the internet on a daily basis and are influencing older generations in a way no other generation has done before.

It is estimated that about 40 per cent, or around 366 million Chinese born in the period 1980-97, fall into this category. Raised in a time of great social and economic change in China and lavished with overwhelming attention from doting parents as a result of China's one-child policy, Generation Y has emerged as a well-educated, highly opinionated segment of the workforce. They are also prone to be fickle in their tastes, less bound to company loyalty and less deferential to hierarchy and authority than their parents and grandparents. Moving readily from conservative work environments, they are constantly in search of better learning and career development opportunities in more creative and entrepreneurial environments. In particular, they are the force behind the social media revolution in China, the preference for online and mobile video rather than terrestrial (state-controlled) TV and online retailing.

As broadband and satellite technology extends deeper into the inner and western provinces, the influence of Generation Y will grow even further. Research suggests that social media plays an even more important role in China as compared to the US, Japan and Europe. As the first Chinese generation to grow up in a globalised world, Generation Y experienced foreign brands for the first time online, not by using Facebook or Twitter (blocked in China) but through local equivalents such as Renren and Sina Weibo. According to several studies, China is now the second largest online shopping market in the world.

Researching market cultures and trends

What does all this mean for Western companies? First, companies can no longer view China as a single market. Targeting the masses will no longer work. Over the next decade, the game will change to take account of the emergence of different categories of consumers and their own sense of their differences and individuality. Companies will have to make extensive research of individual market cultures and trends across the entire 'federation' of China's provinces and age groups to connect with each group and to stand out from competitors. Understanding China as a homogeneous culture or business environment, with shared traditions, customs and etiquettes, will not be sufficient to penetrate successfully into the second-tier and third-tier cities of the central and western provinces.

But then China never was a single, unified country of tastes, history, religion, beliefs and customs. From Xinjiang in the west to Manchuria in the northeast, China has always been an extraordinary patchwork quilt of cultures and peoples. In this sense, the country could be considered as a version of Asia as whole, with its many related but unique cultures, traditions and ways of doing business.

For those entering the China market or seeking to expand, the conclusion is clear. Although there may appear to be a global segment of aspiring middle class consumers in the country, local market conditions and characteristics in each of the regions and their cities will continue to challenge Western companies. This challenge will extend to learning the appropriate business behaviour, culture and ways to build business relationships in each of China's provinces and often in second- or third-tier cities too.

Instead of just adopting a one-size-fits-all approach to Chinese business culture, moving traditional product categories or engaging in practices developed in home markets, Western companies will have to focus more on enhancing their knowledge of each particular market and the value they bring to local consumers. Only by doing this will they be able to build successful partnerships, increase economies of scale and strive to maximise returns in these new markets.

Branding and expectations

Understanding the differences in consumer and business behaviour by city tier, and also by geography, will also allow you to develop effective entry/expansion plans, marketing campaigns and brand strategies. While several studies have focused on specific groups of Chinese consumers including women and Generation Y, they have been limited in geographic coverage and sample validity. Most of the studies have focused on the inhabitants and their consumer behaviour in a few big cities. Research to date has not fully explored the regional variations in consumer characteristics and their marketing implications. As Western companies continue to increase their stake in the country, understanding of regional differences in culture, lifestyle and consumer purchasing power is critical to assess local market demand accurately and to enact effective business strategies.

Countless stories have emerged of major Western companies that have failed in China, or sought a local partner after highly expensive mistakes because they couldn't read or understand the precise local market culture. In other words, the drive to understand and leverage the business culture of China must become even more laser-focused on the gathering of market research, local knowledge and competitive intelligence. It doesn't matter if you are a senior executive in a Western company, a partner in online retailing or an entrepreneur — ultimately you will have to target your brands to narrower consumer segments and offer products that are specifically tailored to local culture and tastes. This means that you will have to get to know the local Chinese provincial or city culture (or more likely, cultures) in far more depth than is currently contemplated in most Western companies, including those with a major presence in the country.

Over the years, I have advised several multinational companies based in Hong Kong. One of these is a major retail company with a leading position in its market throughout Asia. For the last decade the company has been trying to establish its successful Asia-wide brand and store concepts in China. However, it still hasn't turned a profit on years of investment and strategic positioning. A few years ago, it began to group its stores in China into four regional clusters roughly equivalent to the points of the compass but it still hasn't fully succeeded in aligning its products and brand with the culture, lifestyle, purchasing power and tastes of each cluster. And this is a Hong Kong Chinese company with localised Chinese management.

How much harder it is for non-Chinese companies to penetrate such a variegated and challenging market. Brands extended across too many consumer segments and price points may struggle to defend their market position. Hard though the transition can be, at some point companies that have focused on maximising their brands' scale will have to adopt a model based on a portfolio of more targeted brands or sub-brands to connect with different consumer segments and much more precise knowledge of local culture, lifestyle and aspirations.

If you want to succeed in the markets of China, embrace their diversity and get to know everything you can about the shared business culture and etiquette that applies almost everywhere in China. At the same time, you should also get to know the culture, tastes and behaviour with local characteristics of your market(s), because they will play a decisive role in whether you and your company succeed in China.

Drivers of consumer behaviour

If there is any difference in the pursuit of quality of life between East and West, it lies in the obsessive determination of Asian people to achieve success along with all the visible trappings of that success. In addition to saving money for their children's education (the best that can be bought), they strive to buy an apartment or house, a prestigious car or two, an overseas family holiday, as well as brand-name bags, jewellery, watches, clothes and electronic goods that reflect their social status.

China is no exception to this rule. Generally speaking, the rapidly growing Chinese middle classes believe that, with the right competitive tools, they will find an opportunity to transform their lives. Most Chinese regard a higher educational degree as one of the most important drivers of economic and social success. Even before their children are born, they are being allocated schools and budgets and possible university places. This devotion to education derives from family ambition, competition, tradition and culture as well as a deep-rooted respect for knowledge and expertise. Education leads to social recognition, which is a major priority in Chinese life. The number and quality of brand-name products owned by any single individual is further testimony to this need for social recognition.

However, this is not simply a story of social arrival. The purchasing power and sophistication of what is loosely called the Chinese middle class (which economists forecast to jump by a hundred million in the next few years) varies enormously, as the maps at the beginning of this chapter suggest — from province to province and city tier to city tier. A penchant for luxury and international brands is clearly discernible in the inhabitants of the coastal cities. These members of the Chinese middle class might be said to have 'arrived'.

However, they almost certainly share the conviction of the less affluent and more modest majority of middle-class Chinese that they are on a journey, a continuous struggle upward, and they are acutely aware that everything might be lost in a second. Civic institutions are unreliable in China, property law is unreliable, there is no political representation, and the social safety net for such issues as health and employment is very weak. At the bottom end, those farmers now joining the endless migration trail to the third-tier cities have no land title to fall back on.

The 'arrivistes' are therefore driven towards obtaining various accepted icons of middle-class status.

International luxury brands such as Gucci, Louis Vuitton, Chanel, Mercedes-Benz, BMW, Rolex, Cartier, all are at the top of Chinese consumers' shopping lists, along with Cuban cigars, membership of private clubs (exclusivity is highly valued), hotel and airline rewards programmes, and the latest Apple or Samsung phones or laptops. However, such items are very expensive and the disposable incomes of most incipient middle-class Chinese remain low. They will therefore only choose one of these items, or more likely a Chinese equivalent. The crucial factor is whether the item will help a middle-class family create something sustainable. In China's uncertain social and political climate, their main emotional drive is to remain within the charmed middle-class circle and not drop out.

I recently took part in a familiarisation tour of Chinese CEOs from Beijing to the UK, and everywhere we went, from Cambridge University to London, the main drive of their questions was how inheritance and succession issues are handled in the UK. In other words, they wanted to know how to hold on to what they have, including and above all their social status. It is true that some members of China's upper-middle class are becoming more modern and international. Their children are being educated at schools and universities all over the world. They now travel in huge numbers, not only to traditional shopping destinations like Hong Kong but also to Paris, Vancouver, Sydney and Rio de Janeiro. They are increasingly global and their children in particular are extremely internet-savvy and often speak very good English. However, this does not necessarily mean that they are becoming more Western.

If you want to successfully position your company, your brand and products for the Chinese middle-class market, you must understand that the primary driving force is social advancement allied to sustainability — and, for the vast majority of new middle-class entrants, affordability too. Most Chinese will not buy expensive foreign products for the home because they are not visible signs of status. However, those that can truly afford them do seek out high visibility foreign products, particularly if they can show the owner's status in an understated or subtle way. To some extent, the Confucian respect for modesty and the Middle Way still affects Chinese business and shopping behaviour. Similarly, a product that projects reliability and longevity, such as a diamond engagement ring, finds increasing favour in the Chinese marketplace.

On present trends, there could be more than two billion Asians in middle-class households by 2020. In China alone, there could be over 670 million 'middle class consumers' (loosely called), which amounts to almost half the population. As a member of a Western company, you cannot afford to be left behind. You must fully educate yourself on the beliefs, habits, traditions, background and tastes of your Chinese business clients, partners and consumers, learn how to interact and communicate with them, tailor your products and brands accordingly and be ready to build long-term relationships in the cities and provinces where they live.

Action points

1. Study the two maps of China in this chapter and try to learn some of the relative GDPs of individual provinces by 2020. Choose four different areas of the country, cover the map of comparative country GDPs, and jot down some country comparisons for individual Chinese provinces.

2. Look at the comparative map again and use internet research to make a list of 6 first-tier, 10 second-tier and 15 third-tier cities by population size. Note where they are located.

3. List out some of the main differences between Generation Y and their parents and grandparents in they way they approach life and business.

4. Consider why regional differences in culture, lifestyle and consumer purchasing power are critical to assess local market demand in China. Why will these factors affect your branding, products and marketing?

CHAPTER FOUR

THE BASICS OF CHINESE BUSINESS ETIQUETTE

I READ SOMEWHERE RECENTLY that the best way to approach the differences of culture and etiquette in Asia between different countries, and to avoid confusion with Western cultural norms, is to group Asian countries under their primary means of eating: Chopsticks or Hands.

The Chopsticks countries include China, Hong Kong SAR, Japan, Korea, Taiwan, Singapore as well as the overseas Chinese in general. They are characterised by their governing Confucian approach to doing business.

Hands countries, by contrast, include those largely Islamic peoples and nations that regard eating with the left hand as unclean and therefore use the right hand to eat. These cultures include Malaysia, Indonesia, southern Thailand and Myanmar and are characterised by their adherence to deep spiritual beliefs.

The problem with such an arbitrary division of cultures is that it is both misleading and condescending. According to the Chopsticks school of thought, the use of chopsticks in these countries reflects a non-rational or illogical cultural trait because eating with chopsticks is not the easiest, most hygienic or elegant way of consuming food. The Hands school of thought ventured that, although eating with the right hand suggested deep spiritual beliefs, it was also an uncomfortable and irrational habit.

Neither Western commentator thought fit to point out that chopsticks were the logical answer to eating from a rice bowl and transferring delicate pieces of food to that bowl from communal dishes in the centre of the table. Nor did they remark that the Koran places a special emphasis on community and family, hence communal eating that allows for food to be wrapped in breads.

Quite apart from the cultural superiority such generalisations assume, these arbitrary divisions confuse more than they inform. It is true that various Asian countries often have different cultures with aspects of etiquette that are uniquely theirs. But as a general rule, it is true to say that almost all Asian cultures have more deep-seated and widespread spiritual or traditional beliefs than Western ones. In terms of business etiquette, this often translates into a higher degree of formality, more gestures of respect, and more concern with correct titles, among other refined manners.

Such questions go to the heart of this book. For what differentiates almost all Western business people who are successful in China, as well as almost all successful business travellers, is that they have learned to see the culture of the country in which they are a visitor from a viewpoint other than their own, more Western-oriented culture.

They are able to enter into the spirit of China through willingness, preparation, emotional intelligence, empathy and lateral thinking. To take a simple example, ask yourself whether you would be flattered to be called 'primitive hunter-gatherers' because you still eat with a knife and fork. Or whether you would be happy to be termed 'inelegant' because you were hooked on McDonalds burgers (which you eat with your hands, by the way).

These are not incidental questions. Countless surveys have concluded that the way you present yourself in the office and work environment accounts for almost 80 per cent of business success. Business is often based on first and ongoing impressions, body language, common courtesies and attention to small details. How much truer is this in the Chinese context, where fitting in and collective cohesion are at a premium, as well as building long-lasting relationships and saving face (avoiding embarrassment) at all costs.

China is a vast, diverse and complex country that is undergoing rapid change. Most provinces of China share beliefs and customs in common. However, there are often important gradations from province to province, just as there are subtle differences within those provinces based on relative wealth and stage of development, ethnic and religious groups, shared history, geographical area, the assumptions of business, corporate and political élites, and so on.

There can be no one-size-fits-all approach to Chinese business etiquette. It would also be ridiculous to assume that the cultural and national traits identified in this chapter apply to every single individual from the country and or indeed from a particular province. As we saw in Chapter Three there are huge differences in sophistication, openness to international influences, level of education and access to the latest technology in first-tier, second-tier and the interior cities. As also explained in Chapter Three, there are radical differences in the attitude towards work and family culture among the younger generation (Generation Y), their parents and their grandparents. However, the attempt to make sense of the overall cultural and business environment of China is undoubtedly an essential step towards building a successful business.

The overview of business etiquette that follows is an attempt to provide a better understanding of China business practices while helping you avoid unnecessary embarrassment or giving offence. They are stepping-stones into worlds that will require much more detailed attention as your business develops. Once you have absorbed this introduction to Chinese business etiquette, it will be time to go deeper into those aspects that will particularly impact and promote your business for the long term.

General etiquette rules

Asian countries are considered to be high-context cultures. In a high-context culture many things are left unsaid, letting the culture do the explaining. The Chinese believe they must know and trust someone before they are willing to enter into a business agreement or make a business decision. Communication is largely indirect and reliant on tone of voice, gestures, behaviour at formal occasions and respect systems. A straightforward 'yes' or 'no' is not usually offered to a direct question. On the other hand, the Chinese are often persistent, if passive negotiators.

Westerners largely come from low-context cultures. They communicate directly, get to the point and move on quickly in business so as not to waste time, even if they don't know someone well. Action and getting down to business are viewed as priorities, which often means that high-context Chinese view their Western counterparts as impatient, insincere or casual. Or all three together!

Of course there is nothing wrong with getting to the point in business negotiations. However, in China it is generally considered more appropriate to take these negotiations step-by-step, drawing in and referring to each person or department responsible for each aspect of the deal. When all parties are fully convinced that their concerns are covered, the trust is built that ensures a long-term relationship.

For those who are unwilling or unable to spend sufficient time in China to achieve this, a parachute in-and-out visit will not be of much assistance. It is vital that your company's local representative maintains ongoing contact and interaction with your proposed partner, and that trust is developed to the extent that your Chinese partner or client is assured of the total value of the deal in the long term. For Chinese business people, this is far preferable to short-term business deals that always have to begin again from scratch when the next step is negotiated (the Western 'economics-trumps-relationships' approach).

Here are some of the more obvious business etiquette tips that are generally applicable across China.

Introductions

Meeting and greeting

In Chinese society first meetings are expected to be fairly formal. An excessive amount of friendliness or familiarity is not encouraged, since it runs against the traditional Confucian respect for social standing. In meetings with business or government officials, the atmosphere may even seem slightly frosty or at least non-committal, which again is the Confucian norm. All you have to do is to mirror the attitude and be polite. If it's a large reception you may have to introduce yourself to the other guests but at a smaller gathering or a meeting with the Chinese team (or between both teams), wait for the host or your Chinese go-between to do the honours.

Greetings are formal and the oldest person is always greeted first. Shaking hands is now routine in Chinese culture, particularly for visits of VIPs, government leaders or senior executives. However, remember that the Chinese are not very comfortable with physical contact in public. The handshake should be strong enough to suggest respect but not too strong in the manner of a George Bush Jr. The Chinese avoid staring straight in the eye and they will expect you to do the same during the introductions and subsequent meeting.

Handshake or bow?

At the initial and indeed at all consequent meetings with your Chinese counterparts, watch out for the Mr. Bean moment. By that I mean being put off by the formality and allowing yourself to be tempted into a vaguely Asian type of bow from the waist. This is not only politically incorrect (it is a Japanese formality) but also unnecessary. The old style of Chinese greeting was to place the left hand over the right fist, bow and shake your hands like a long-lost cousin but nowadays the Chinese will only slightly bow their head as a show of politeness.

I have had some hilarious moments in the foyers of hotels or formal receptions when in my formal suit I have attempted to replace or follow the usual Western handshake with what I thought was a more Chinese bow or even tenting my hands to my forehead as if I was in Thailand. Sometimes my 'Eastern' gestures would work. Usually, I ended up looking like Mr. Bean about to keel over.

The general rule is: stick to the handshake. If you feel confident, a slight bow of the head can accompany the handshake. If you visit a university or factory or conference, you or your group may be greeted with applause: simply applaud back. It is simply a form of greeting, largely adopted by the communist party, and you are basically applauding the communal effort. As always, a concession to local traditions is often the key to successful business relations in China.

In general, the Chinese are understated. They do not appreciate body contact with strangers such as back slapping or touching, clicking fingers, pointing with index fingers (use an open hand facing downwards), whistling, legs on the table, placing your feet in the vicinity of someone's head, leaving hands in pockets or sucking in air loudly to express surprise.

Presenting your business card

This is a subject that creates a minefield of misunderstandings. However, there is no reason why this should be so. Presenting your credentials is an obvious way of initiating business contact in both East and West. Business people all over the world send out individual and company portfolios and resumés, create websites and use social media such as Facebook and LinkedIn, to initiate business.

The only major difference is that Westerners tend to be more relaxed about introducing themselves, or at least less formal, and do not use business cards much. Even when they do, the cards are often handed out in a cocktail party way with one hand on a glass of something and the other flicking the card into a convenient side pocket.

China is very different in this regard. It is generally considered that a business card represents a person's identity. The card is literally the *face* of you and your business: who you are and what position you hold. Just as we wouldn't mistreat a face by scribbling on it, or by offering it with a flick of the hand, or by dumping it into a back pocket wallet to be sat on, so too the Chinese business card demands respect.

There is a rite that follows on a first meeting in China, just after the handshake and initial exchange of names. That is the exchange of business cards. And just as in any rite, there are simple rules to observe.

First, make sure that the business card has all your details and is printed in English on one side and Chinese on the other. Make sure the characters are simplified Chinese for mainland China (Hong Kong, Malaysia and Indonesia use traditional Chinese characters). Take advice on the Chinese characters for your name and title with the most auspicious connotations. The Chinese are often deeply impressed by 'lucky' characters and 'lucky' numerals.

In general, business cards have much greater cultural significance in China than in Western culture. They provide information about the group to which you belong, where you stand in the hierarchy and therefore how much respect should be shown to you. Not presenting a business card at a business meeting is tantamount to not shaking hands at a Western business meeting. It sometimes causes irreparable damage.

Second, always stand up to exchange cards. The cards themselves should be meticulously clean and if possible produced from an elegant cardholder. Bent or smudged or worn-out cards will not do. Present your card with both thumbs holding the card in front of you, NOT in one hand as if you are about to play poker. The Chinese translation should be on the upper side of the card. If required (and it usually is, since everyone at the meeting will come armed with their own cards), continue to present your cards one-by-one, individual-by-individual, using both hands if possible. Remember you have to accept the other person's business card in the same respectful manner, so if you are new to the game, practise with your colleagues until you get the rhythm and the presentation fluent.

Third, observe some simple 'dos' and 'don'ts'. Don't toss the cards about in any manner. Don't place a stack of them on the table and ask people to help themselves. Don't put the card away in an inner pocket, or worse, lose it somewhere in your trousers or skirt pockets. Leave it out with the others on the tabletop or in your hands as the meeting proceeds so that you can refer to it (your Chinese counterparts will find this respectful and take note).

Don't write comments on anyone else's business card in their presence, such as when the client is available, next meeting, mobile number, etc., since this is equivalent to writing on their face. Many Chinese hand out their business cards as if there were no tomorrow. Don't be left out. Take an ample supply of cards with you to every meeting. You will use many more of them than in your home country.

Correct manner of address

Many Westerners are put off by the number of names the Chinese seem to have, and the order in which they are offered. Even after all these years, I still sometimes confuse the surname with the (usually two) forenames. You will see that Chinese names are usually presented as a surname followed by two linked forenames on their business card. The general rule of thumb is to use the surname with an honorific on first meeting (e.g. the male Chin, Tahn Joo on the business card would translate to 'Mr. Chin' in conversation). Never use the first name on the card to address the person, and always try to use Mr. or Ms., Miss or Mrs. When introducing VIP guests, the Chinese usually use full titles and company names, such as Doctor Michael Williams, CEO of United International Bank (Chinese tend to be very respectful about education and qualifications). You should do the same for the Chinese.

Increasing numbers of Chinese are now travelling all round the world and frequently deal with foreigners. In this case, they may use a Western name like Mike or Jeff. However, don't plunge in on first-name terms until invited to do so. If your Chinese counterparts want to move to a first-name basis, they will advise you which name to use. Avoid using the term 'comrade' in any context. Not only is it inappropriate in a Westerner's mouth, but also it is rarely used in modern China and has a variety of negative connotations. The good news is that, like the Overseas Chinese, Mainland Chinese have a strong sense of humour when they feel comfortable in a relationship. Be prepared to laugh at yourself when you have overcome the first hurdles.

Saving or losing face
In such a collectivist and hierarchical society, it is essential that outsiders avoid causing a Chinese to

lose face at any time. The Chinese largely rely on facial expression, tone of voice and posture to tell them what someone feels. If someone disagrees with what another person in a meeting has said, that person will remain quiet. This gives respect to the other person, whereas speaking out would make both parties lose face.

The direct eye contact used by a Westerner to show interest may be taken as an aggressive tactic by the Chinese, who will not look you in the eye when you are talking to them since it is considered rude. Frowning while someone is speaking is also interpreted as a sign of disagreement. Therefore, most Chinese maintain an impassive expression when listening.

This obliqueness is very hard for individualist Westerners to understand, but it stems from the unwillingness to upset the collective harmony. Obliqueness and respect for harmony are hallmarks of Chinese culture. Contradicting someone openly, criticising them in front of someone else, putting them in awkward situations or patronising them are a sure way to lose business. They make it impossible to save face. Always *give* face through sincere compliments, showing respect or doing something that raises self-esteem.

Women in business

It is a commonly held belief in Western countries that gender equality has a poor record in Asian cultures. Business women are supposedly given far less respect and attention then in many Western countries. Confucianism dictates that women are subservient to and should always

THE BASICS OF CHINESE BUSINESS ETIQUETTE

obey 'father, husband and son'. Women in China have long been held back by the lack of professional, political and educational opportunities on offer to men.

However, these attitudes have been slowly changing over the past decades. In business, women have achieved the status of honorary men. Even though women's presence is still rare in government circles, women are rapidly moving into leadership positions elsewhere. It is worth noting that almost 50 per cent of the senior executives in China are women. Don't assume that the Chinese woman in the boardroom is a junior manager about to pour the tea.

Chinese do direct some resistance to women in business but this is mainly at local women, and in particular at 'strong women' who might be seen to upset the normal male succession in family businesses. It is not usually aimed at Western business women. This is possibly because the Chinese see women as equal to men because of their emotional intelligence. Women are increasingly perceived as smart negotiators, softly spoken and persuasive, good at instinctive reactions and listening, more able than men to seek out common ground and explore client's needs, more patient and curious about other people and their lifestyles.

In other words, Western women have an increased chance of business success in China because they rely more on the 'feel' and 'context' of a business situation, rather than on immediate gains and direct outcomes. In countries like Japan and South Korea, where business is still highly male dominated, women executives still have to pay extra attention to demonstrating their seniority through the local etiquette protocols. But Western businesswomen whose behaviour accords with Chinese male preconceptions can be and often are readily accepted. Equally, Western businessmen should not treat Chinese women in business as any different from their male counterparts and should adopt the same business etiquette as they would with a male Chinese counterpart.

Meetings

It is usual that your Chinese intermediary or member of your team will arrange meetings and appointments on your behalf. More and more Chinese company officials are able to communicate in some form of English, and in the élite business, technology and government circles of cities like Beijing and Shanghai, many high-flying Chinese are now bilingual. However, it is always best to bring your own interpreter (and sometimes even two for delicate negotiations, to check on each other). This will help you understand the essential subtleties and face-saving ploys of the meeting.

Punctuality and presenting

It is a sign of respect all over China to be on time for appointments. If the traffic is bad, as it is bound to be in the numerous rapidly growing cities of the country, don't over-schedule and always call ahead if late. This saves your face (it is your hosts' country and their traffic problems) and also that of your local partner.

In accordance with Chinese business protocol, enter the room in order of seniority with the most senior person going ahead first. The Chinese will immediately identify that person as the leader of the group. That same person should open and lead the meeting. The Chinese will not expect the most senior person to make the presentation, so make sure that the key points of your message are explained by your executives and that you simply draw the presentation to a close.

In Chinese etiquette, the presenter is the one in charge and holds the floor without any interruptions or questions from anyone, so warn the liveliest members of your team to keep a low profile while someone else is talking. It is important to treat every Chinese in the room with the same respect, because the opaque and complex nature of Chinese organisations means that it is often very unclear as to who will make the final decisions. Sometimes the decision-maker is not even in the room; the Chinese present will have to report to him or her. Therefore, treat everybody with equal respect and be ready to repeat your presentation several times over to people higher in the organisation.

For a fuller discussion of presentation and leadership styles, see Chapter Eight. Suffice it to say here that communications should be simple, clear and jargon-free. Once they have absorbed what you have to say, the Chinese should be allowed to leave the room first.

Business attire

As a general rule, play safe and be conservative, with suits, ties and tie-up shoes for men, and unrevealing semi-formal suits and dresses for women. A business meeting, lunch or dinner or even drinking coffee together tends to be rather formal, at least at the outset, with handshakes, an exchange of business cards, discreet inspections and elaborate courtesies about who is paying (usually the host), and so on.

In warmer parts of this vast country with its many microclimates and huge distances from north to south, a smart shirt and tie and slacks or even an open-necked shirt may be permissible. However, check what business people are wearing before you make your choice. A suit may still be preferred in tropical, heavily air-conditioned Guangzhou or even Shanghai during the summer, depending on the industry and sector.

Personal branding

Many Western business people going into Asia forget that one of the most essential ways to open doors and forge lasting business relationships is personal branding. That may sound strange, as if you have to become a Richard Branson or Steve Jobs to succeed. But it's amazing how many people fall down when it comes to projecting themselves and their company.

Part of the challenge is communication: how to speak clearly and at a regular, slower pace in a foreign culture without complicating your language. You have to make sure you're understood. But there's more to it than that. Personal branding goes to the heart of what you are trying to sell or promote: You!

If you walk through almost any of the great cities of China from Chongqing to Tianjin, from Shenzhen to Dalian, you will be knocked out by the sheer amount of visual stimulus: stylish architecture, huge billboards with beautiful actors or actresses and singers, models, top-of-the-line cars, world-class cosmetics and fashion.

The numerous provinces and cities of China often have youthful and dynamic cultures. The younger generation usually form a majority of their populations. Their idols fill the airwaves and the TV channels. Everywhere, stylishness and modernity are on display. Therefore, those who desire success in the marketplaces of China should sit up and take notice.

A major element of the Chinese emphasis on context for assessing business partners is *what you look like*. That may sound superficial but it's true. The visual first impression you give in what are increasingly smart, sophisticated, cosmopolitan and cultured Chinese business circles is what really counts. Your face, your clothing, your body language and your speech are all part of what a Chinese counterpart will conclude about you. This may sound like the Hollywood hang-up on image. It may strike you as nothing to do with someone who is selling USBs in Yunnan province.

But in China, as in much of Asia, the visual goes beyond simply image. The good (well educated, professional) impression you make is often the entry point for further conclusions about you, such as your truthfulness, diligence, kindness, intelligence and loyalty. These values will form part of the impression the Chinese make as to whether they can work with you. In almost every part of China, this unspoken feeling is what cements the relationship. The image you project will see you categorised into boxes labelled 'social class', 'education', 'potential' and '*I want to be seen with you*'.

So if you are entering China markets for the first time, and want to up your game, just remember that if you ask a Chinese person's opinion about a friend or a potential employee, they will often say, 'They *look* like a good or clever or trustworthy person.'

The good news is that this emphasis is on appearance doesn't mean that you have to undergo plastic surgery! You just have to take care with your personal presentation. Go to the gym and lose some pounds, sort out your wardrobe, get well scrubbed and regularly moisturised, drop the biro and invest in a Mont Blanc, buy a good watch and put away the Swatch. Each of these details will be quickly assessed and noted as part of your personal branding. Each of them will mark you out as being 'worth it'.

No one has ever been looked down upon for dressing up a bit or dressing slightly more conservatively. In China, a 'low level person' is unshaven or wearing a check shirt and baggy chinos or a revealing beach-type dress at a business meeting. If you want to gain millionaire status in China, you have to be on the money. You have to get the rules. And the number one rule is good personal branding.

The language barrier

In many Asian countries, English is reasonably or well spoken as a second language (first language in Singapore). However, in a vast and multi-layered, still largely rural China, this might not always be the case. In particular, English is less spoken outside the principal cities and the signage is almost entirely in Chinese script with no English translation in sight.

You should assess the likelihood of communication difficulties beforehand, particularly if highly technical matters or delicate negotiations are involved, and appoint a trustworthy and recommended interpreter such as a local marketing officer attached to home country embassies or consulates.

It is best to discuss the necessity for an interpreter with your local contacts, such as your local partner, agent or distributor, who may well be able to act as interpreters and guides themselves if required. They will also help you avoid giving offence by taking an interpreter along to a meeting when the Chinese party speaks and understands English well. An increasing number of Chinese are studying English at home or at a language school, so they may well understand more English than they reveal. This means that sensitive information should not be discussed in front of Chinese observers even when they appear not to understand. Key selection criteria for an agent or partner should include their ability to communicate and manage relationships across the East-West cultural divide and to understand your sensitivities. It is vital to take time to find the right partner.

Visitors to China trade fairs should avoid hiring interpreters who offer their services at the gates of the fair. They are not dependable. It is better to find one beforehand from the recommended list of the trade fair websites or by word of mouth from a trusted source within the country, such as a local agent, distributor or expat 'old hand'.

Business entertainment

One of the most popular traditions in China is inviting a business associate to dinner. It doesn't matter whether you are a visitor from a far country or a regular foreigner in their local or city business circles — building or cementing a business relationship is achieved through out-of-business-hours social activities such as dinners, or more usually eight-course or more banquets (eight is lucky, nine is for 'the emperor', but some banquets can run to at least twenty dishes). If you arrive a little early, your Chinese hosts will usually be there and there will be an opportunity for social chat and introductions. As with everything in China, there are certain cultural niceties to observe.

Table manners

If you are being hosted in a Chinese restaurant, as is very likely, the basic rule is to watch what your host does and do likewise. Don't just sit down but wait to be directed to your seat. Often the foreign guest is placed in a seat of honour in the middle of the table, facing the door and opposite the host.

If it's a Chinese meal, there will be a series of dishes placed on the central revolving dais. Both spoons and chopsticks will be available next to your plate and bowl. Use the chopsticks (if you are able) to pick morsels from the central plateau and place them in your bowl. Return the chopsticks to the curved rest every now and then, but don't lay them across your bowl. The rice comes later, so you are free to use the bowl for eating and to place any bones on your side plate. Only begin eating after the host has begun, and if you are offered a morsel by your host or another Chinese, be sure to accept it and eat it with or without rice.

However, don't attempt to finish all the dishes on the table or go for a second serving, and only use your spoon to scoop up food if and when necessary. Eating everything implies there is not enough food, quite apart from you appearing greedy. Conversely, eating too much during the first courses may mean that you have to refuse the later ones, which also appears rude. It's best to sample lightly. Each course may be announced with a toast of *Gan-bei* ('cheers') that is echoed round the table. Raise your glass at the others and join in the toast. Similarly, raise your glass modestly if you are toasted. You may offer a toast yourself if the occasions demands, but only at the end of the meal.

Mainland Chinese can be big drinkers at banquets, so be on your guard for excessive tippling. If tea is poured into your cup by others, tent your index and second finger on the table top and tap them a couple of times to express thanks. This finger tapping comes from a long tradition or saying thank you. Legend says that the tradition originated during the Qing Dynasty, when the emperor went incognito among his people to find out how they really lived. Part of his disguise was to pour tea for his courtiers, who wanted to *kowtow* (prostrate themselves) before him. But since this would reveal his identity, he told them to gently tap three fingers on the table. The middle finger represented the bowed head and the other two the prostrate arms. Finally, don't insist on paying. That would definitely cause the host to lose face!

If you are invited to a private house, consider it a great honor and be sure to arrive on time. Remove your shoes before entering the house and present a small gift to the hostess. Eat well to demonstrate that you are enjoying the food, but again you don't have to finish everything on the table. Overabundance shows the status of the host.

Conversation and business

If you do business in China, it is essential to remember that the Chinese approach is not necessarily direct and 'let's get down to business', especially when meeting socially (for example, for dinner). Chinese expect the approach to be indirect, even circuitous, and above all based on getting to know the Western counterpart in order to build a relationship of trust, credibility and obligation.

Since Chinese culture is also so family-oriented, this often means that enquiries and discussion about family and social background/circumstances, home and hobbies, take precedence over direct business negotiations. At a first business meeting, especially a formal lunch or dinner, business is often not expected to be the primary topic. Chinese business partners want to get to know you, not your bottom line. They want to know if there is likely to be longevity in the relationship, if they can get on with you, if you have the ability to work in harmony with their business and social culture.

Conversations often include discussions about the food. In fact, the Chinese love to talk about food! You can make a very good impression by saying the food is delicious (*meiwei*), or by discussing the flavours, the method of cooking, or what is grown locally. Whatever you might truly feel, don't turn your nose up at anything or ask what on earth it is. Have a few words of Chinese. Even 'thank you' or 'yes' and 'no' gets you a long way in business. Be complimentary, for example, about the local transport, culture, temple you've seen, city's modernity, etc. Show politeness to the waiters, even if they're not polite to you or don't conform to your standards. It also doesn't do any harm to enquire about your host's family, travel plans, local village or city or anything that shows you are educated and interested.

If you're going to a private home, arrive on time and bring a small but delicate gift (for business gift-giving, see Chapter Seven). Most Chinese homes have a small lobby or cupboard where outdoor shoes are to be left and slippers put on. Don't walk straight onto the clean floor!

Gifts and festivals

The Chinese lunar calendar is full of festive occasions. Once you are accepted as being a long-term business partner, it is inevitable that you will be asked to attend some of these occasions. If you attend, just remember some basic rules and prepare yourself beforehand.

If it's Chinese New Year and you are invited to someone's house on the third or fourth day (two days are for the extended family network), take along some carefully wrapped candies or chocolate or a basket of fruit. Red and gold are auspicious colours for Chinese New Year and other seasons, so choose red or gold wrapping paper. Gifts for other occasions can include alcohol such as plum wine for women and cognac for men, flowers (not white since they suggest mourning), and general delicacies, chocolates or cakes.

Since it's an auspicious festive season, you can also give red packets with freshly minted banknotes to employees, service staff at your apartment, juniors and children. Never give clocks or watches, as they are associated with death, or anything that cuts, because scissors and knives suggest terminating the relationship. Also avoid anything that comes in fours (the word for four is similar to the word for death in Mandarin). However, giving eight of something is considered extremely lucky. Gifts are not usually opened when received and they may be refused up to three times before being accepted.

Drinking and karaoke

In some Asian cultures, relationship building may well be dependent on the amount of alcohol consumed during evening 'entertainment' sessions. This is particularly true in China, Japan and Korea. Since some of the local drinks, such as Chinese rice wine, can be up to 50 per cent or more proof, it is best to be extremely careful about getting drunk (sipping beer or giving a medical reason for drinking soft drinks are acceptable alternatives).

Don't comment or even feign surprise if your counterpart becomes drunk, and don't mention it the next day. Not all Chinese approve of drinking alcohol. Devout Buddhists don't drink it and you shouldn't if your Chinese colleagues abstain. In particular, women should abstain in public places.

Evening drinking is invariably followed or accompanied by karaoke sessions or visits to karaoke bars. Visiting Westerners should expect to take part in these as an integral part of relationship building. My solution is to prepare in advance a small repertoire of two or three numbers that you can repeat everywhere. I have lost count of the number of times I have rolled out 'New York, New York' or 'Don't Cry for Me Argentina' in Hong Kong, Seoul, Tokyo, Beijing and Manila. My renditions didn't improve, but the relationships did.

Action points

1. If you are not entirely clear what is meant by low-context and high-context cultures, go back over this chapter and list out some of the major differences in business approach between your customary business circles and what you may encounter in Chinese business circles.

2. Consider how you might improve your personal branding to make a good impression on your Chinese partners. What practical steps can you take to raise your game?

3. Think of an occasion on which you might have prevented your Chinese counterpart from losing face, or yourself from losing face, and consider how you might have done things differently to avoid any suggestion of offence or negatively impacting a business negotiation.

4. Go back over the Chinese business etiquette tips and practice with a colleague how they might be applied in action: for example, the exchange of business cards, introducing yourself and addressing your counterpart, accepting a toast at a business meal, and so on.

5. Actively seek advice on local business customs, etiquette and mistakes to avoid from your China consultant, local partner or members of your local team. This learning process takes time, effort and sensitivity.

CHAPTER FIVE

HOW TO NETWORK SUCCESSFULLY

THE MAIN BUSINESS-RELATED cross-cultural difference between the West and the Chinese is the significance of the long-term business relationship. What the Chinese call *guanxi* (relationship) is at the heart of Chinese business deals. When Chinese business people meet for the first time, they begin to immediately build guanxi. They will probably spend many hours drinking tea or discussing subjects that seem 'non-business' to Westerners. Chinese use this process to assess people they might like to work with. This often makes results-driven Westerners very impatient.

However, having a good network of connections in China is the most important element of business success. Every Chinese cultivates his or her own network of personal relationships in business, by which is meant networks with obligations. For Westerners too, guanxi relationships and networking often serve to smooth out operations but there are crucial differences between the Western idea of networking and building relationships and the Chinese system of guanxi. It is therefore essential to work initially through an intermediary who cannot only make a formal introduction and vouch for the reliability of your company but is also someone who teaches you how the guanxi system works.

The basics of guanxi

An understanding of guanxi in Chinese culture is an essential requirement for both doing business in China and with Chinese business people you meet online or in your home country. The problem is to know what guanxi really means. I have lost count of the number of times I have heard the word used loosely in speeches or conversation by Western commentators or business people without any specific application. They seem to suggest that simply using the word implies recognition of the difference in how personal interactions work in China from their own country.

The best starting point is to think of Chinese personal relationships as a series of interlocking circles. Immediate family members make up the first circle, then extended family members, then people from the same town or neighbourhood. School and undergraduate guanxi can play an important part in someone's later professional or business life, while more casual acquaintances, local shopkeepers and building attendants can make up a more peripheral outer circle. Since non-Chinese have no guanxi networks in China, they are not part of these charmed circles and by definition will find it difficult to build relationships or connections with the Chinese. The most they can hope for is to become a 'foreign friend'.

That does not mean that you can afford to ignore the guanxi system or treat it as peripheral to doing business in China. In many cases, it is the only way to achieve real business success and therefore has to be approached with commitment and careful study.

Guanxi is a bond of trust and understanding between two individuals that provides the key to networks of professional 'connections' (the literal meaning of the word) and contacts. In order to obtain the key, you have to recognise that the system is built on obligations and favours that play an informal but essential role in Chinese business. Guanxi building is not to be confused with the Chinese social, banqueting and drinking customs that surround and support it, even though these traditional habits of hospitality are used to build the personal connections that the guanxi system eventually benefits. As in many countries in Asia, the personal relationship is vital to the beginning of all serious negotiations in China.

Building relationships

It is sometimes difficult to explain to Westerners that Chinese business deals are more based on relationships than on contracts or actual transactions. For the Westerner, a personal relationship may build up over time in an organic way but the important issue is to sign a contract as the first stage towards completing other possible contracts. However, exactly the opposite applies in China. Only after the process of guanxi building has taken its course and strong personal relationships are achieved will the Chinese party move on to consider a commercial transaction. In other words, the rulebook about not mixing business with pleasure or the personal has to be thrown out of the window. The route to a profitable business relationship in China is usually approached from the opposite direction.

As we shall see in Chapter Six, guanxi and relationship building form the initial steps of a Chinese business negotiation. In Western countries, we usually start a negotiation by outlining our company's history, strengths and capabilities and then move on to what we are offering for sale or what we need in supplier terms. In China, these details are considered of minor importance in comparison to your attitude and character. The Chinese side will always focus on the possibilities of doing business personally rather than on legal terms or binding contracts. However, it would be wrong to think these relationships are considered in an emotional or sentimental way. They are strictly business focused and you may be lulled into a false sense of security by all the talk about families and hobbies, the flattery and smiles during the initial phase of the process.

In fact, the Chinese are very good at passive manipulation and may be quite ruthless in rejecting you once their purposes are fulfilled. You must be careful not to allow your Western business attitude, based largely on a clear offer and a take-it-or-leave approach, to soften so much that you fall completely for Chinese personal charm. On the other hand, you have to accept that good guanxi building is the principal route to business success in China.

Knowing the culture, history and traditions of China and trying to follow Chinese business etiquette as much as possible will certainly help, not least because that will prevent you coming over as a clumsy buffoon. However, real business can only be achieved through guanxi, so if you don't get the system right, you will always be in a position of weakness. This means knowing the right person with whom to build a relationship, who might be important in that person's circle, what you can try to ask for, and what favours and obligations will be requested from you in return.

If you don't participate in this give-and-take system of mutual obligations and favours you may well end up receiving very poor services in return for your high-value resources or assets. The relationship with your Chinese partner may easily turn and you will be quickly portrayed in a negative light as someone who cannot hold up one end of a bargain. On the other hand, if you become adept at building guanxi, it does not necessarily mean that you will be a great business success in China. Building guanxi is certainly one of the important communication and negotiation skills you must commit to learning in China, but don't believe partners or advisors when they tell you that it is the only skill you need to be successful.

There are several negative connotations to guanxi, which will be largely addressed in Chapter Seven. However, the bottom line is that for guanxi to really work for you, you have to be ready to do someone a discernible favour such as helping them with business advice that you would not normally share, or providing a list of schools or universities that you think would be suitable for your Chinese party's children. This will build the right kind of trust and understanding that no amount of carousing or banqueting or karaoke can truly provide, whatever might be said in the manuals of business etiquette. Such customs and etiquettes will certainly give you building blocks for building relationships, but they will be no substitute for the relationship itself, which will be essentially personal. If the person you hired because of their guanxi moves on, so does the relationship. You will have to begin again with someone new and, if you are replaced, that new person will have to build guanxi relations once again from scratch. The connection is exclusively between you and another Chinese person, not between corporations, government departments, subsidiaries or branches.

Similarly, if someone in your network boasts a lot about their guanxi, you can be fairly certain that it is a smokescreen either for their having no great contacts or for their unwillingness to share any of them with you. The most obvious way for a connected person in China to build further on their guanxi is for them to pass on gullible Westerners with ample resources to be exploited by their true guanxi partners. This goes to show that mastering the guanxi system does not necessarily guarantee success. However, if you cannot build personal relationships that have a carefully monitored, in-built system of reciprocal obligations, you will almost certainly fail in China.

Choosing partners

Chinese negotiators build deals on the basis of personal relationships, but these partnerships are not the kind of 50:50 deals that Westerners prefer. The tradition in China is to go for a clear hierarchy, using their knowledge and local connections to take charge or allow you to be the leader, while giving you compliments and face and not much else. Equal partnerships are not common, and if they are found they will have to be negotiated very explicitly from the first meeting.

This builds up a system of obligations or mutual usefulness that may or may not have negative connotations. Your Chinese partners may help you because they plan on you helping them in the future, or they may think you already owe them. Many Western business people operating in China resign themselves to this fact of life, simply using the guanxi network as appropriate while tolerating the occasional empty promises, unequal obligations and failed expectations in order to retain the overall value of the connection.

However, there is a less positive type of guanxi. This is not simply a system dependent on mutual benefit, however onerous the obligation might sometimes be. The more negative form of guanxi is often what puts Western business people off learning anything at all about guanxi and leads them to condemn it as outmoded nonsense that has no place in the modern business world. Simply put, it's a version that encourages cronyism, insider connections, favouritism and peddling of influence. This kind of guanxi involves fixers who don't usually have much to sell, so the fixers offer to sell their connections as a means of solving distribution or supply problems or bureaucratic hindrances. They often help to bring money or assets into China but are of much less help when it comes to building a sustainable business or repatriating profits.

Such fixers with local knowledge were very useful in the days when Chinese commercial law was still chaotic, impenetrable and very loosely applied (if ever).

They pushed bureaucrats to make decisions and ensured they were favourable to the paying party, whether their business clients were from the Mainland, overseas Chinese, Asians or Westerners. However, in the last few years China's central government has been working hard to build a strong legal system and a more transparent regulatory framework. The Third Party Plenum in November 2013, presided over by President Xi Jinping, declared that the eradication of corruption would be a major focus of government reforms going forward and in particular the relationship between guanxi and bribery. The question for Western business people in China is whether they should avoid guanxi altogether. After all, many international experts argue that the system is ineradicably connected with abuse of power and misuse of state assets and should have no place in a modern, ordered China.

The short answer to the question is that you can almost certainly not function without a good guanxi network in China. Without guanxi, you will find it very difficult to find people who are ready and willing to help you build your business. The plugged-in network of guanxi connections enables you to interact with the right decision-makers or resources. However, if you use it as a system of shortcuts to open doors, you may well find that it opens the wrong doors and that the guanxi fixers have simply used their own connections for answers to problems that they can't solve but that they have promised to solve. This kind of fixer can easily end up cheating you of assets, intellectual property or technology in China by promising you powerful introductions or meetings with the right people.

In other words, you have to monitor the role that guanxi plays in your Chinese business. You should avoid using these connections as anything other than value-rich information and networking resources. Excessively friendly gestures may well mean that you are being set up for exaggerated paybacks at some future date. You must carefully reciprocate mutual obligations and not allow yourself to become heavily in guanxi debt.

Moreover, if you ignore the guanxi system and don't hold up your end of the mutual bargain you may also be considered untrustworthy and unworthy of any contracts. You will cut a poor figure and lose considerable face, which means you are no longer a viable business partner to anyone in the network and are a justifiable target for broken promises or theft of assets. Chinese clients can become inexplicably hostile or suddenly scrap a deal just because of some real (or imagined) issue of betrayal of guanxi obligations. So the Golden Rule is to monitor what you owe, and be sure to control what you're supposed to pay back and when.

Strategic alliances

There is a certain tendency in Western business circles to think that anything that varies from best practice as understood and implemented in Western countries such as America or Britain is defective and not to be followed in any circumstances. The general feeling is that eventually all Asian countries, and China in particular, will become more Western and follow due process in terms of law and business behaviour and clear rules and straightforward, enforceable contracts. The thinking is that if you speak slowly and loudly enough and are patient, eventually the Chinese partner will behave more like a Western-educated MBA.

It may be that Generation Y, particularly entrepreneurs working in the digital or creative industries spheres, may be accommodating their business practices more to Western ways of doing things. However, it also appears that their parents are still very happy with the Chinese way of doing business, and they are strongly aware that they have been very successful in business and expanding investment all over the world in the past few years. The Chinese believe this is because they have a strong inclination to build strategic relationships and informal networks — a kind of turbocharged guanxi system with global implications. They are comfortable with this modus operandi and they feel that it has been proven in the marketplace.

As China business continues to expand in the world, it is likely that guanxi will remain part of the Chinese business culture for the foreseeable future. Many Chinese business people express themselves satisfied with the system, even though they are many aspects of Chinese business that they would like to see changed or improved. They want to eradicate the negative aspects of guanxi but not the system itself.

As Chinese social media catches up with and even surpasses that of the West, it is possible that the guanxi-building process will become more codified under law, more transparent and more supported by the latest technology. Already, social media sites are focusing less on entertainment and young people than on actually developing business networks. New technologies will further strengthen the positive sides of guanxi, such as expanding your network, identifying the right business contacts and meeting people within the circle of friends of friends. It is no accident, for example, that many Chinese now use LinkedIn. As the economic and deal-making powers of the Chinese manifest themselves more widely on the global stage, it seems possible that Western companies will have to get used to employing the benefits of the guanxi system in the way they build their China-West strategic alliances and develop their business in China's very localised markets.

Action points

1. Draw a series of interlocking circles or a mind-map of how you perceive the principle elements in the Chinese guanxi system and network, and how they relate to each other.

2. List out some possible ways in which a successful guanxi relationship might work, for example, in terms of personal and helpful favours that do not

constitute a corrupt or illegal relationship. What do you understand by obligations?

3. Write down what you consider to be the Golden Rule (or Rules) of guanxi partnerships and alliances.

4. Consider how the expectations of Generation Y and social media might impact the guanxi system in the future. Will you be prepared?

CHAPTER SIX

THE SECRET TO NEGOTIATIONS

A WESTERNER'S APPROACH TO NEGOTIATION is generally based on logical, sequential steps. For most Chinese, however, negotiation consists of a series of isolated subjects that are finally all connected together based on the value of the total deal. This approach requires persistence and can be a powerful means for Chinese negotiators to secure the point they are seeking, or at least a compromise at the very last moment and even after the negotiations have been 'completed' and the contract signed.

That is perhaps the first and very surprising element of Chinese negotiation for the Western business person to factor into a strategic negotiating plan. You must have such a strategic plan before you begin negotiations or indeed before you launch into business in China.

The time factor

As we have seen in Chapter Five, the guanxi system means that the preparation time needed to develop a suitable network of relationships in China is very long and exhausting. Many Western business people in China complain that the Chinese don't seem to have the same concept of time as we do in the West, or any sense of urgency. This is largely because the Chinese do not view business as being transactions based, a sequence of binding contracts that develop a strong business partnership, but rather in terms of the total value of the relationship in the long term.

In other words, the Chinese negotiate the relationship not the contract. The Chinese view is that if you're still talking, you're still negotiating. This means that Western businesses should not only be prepared to play the negotiating game, but they should also devise a strategic plan that takes the to-and-fro of relationships into account. Always have more to request from the relationship, as the Chinese do, and always have fresh variables to put on the table. If you focus entirely on achieving one set of goals, it is likely that you will lose out over the extended time frame.

Many Western companies still think that negotiations in China can be carried out either over the phone or internet, as they are in their own countries, or at the very most with a quick fly-in-and-out visit prepared by some local partner or distributor or agent on the ground. However, this style of business is almost unknown in China — except perhaps for digital business or online retailing, but even these companies and entrepreneurs must build the personal relationship over time. The requirement for face-to-face meetings extends the time for negotiations, the need for translation, as well as the time necessary to get to know your potential partner. China is a marathon, not a hundred metre dash, and your negotiations are likely to take place over a much longer period of time than in the West.

Guanxi and negotiation

The business of building a network of counterbalancing relationships and social connections is another necessary part of the negotiating process, and needs a lot of care and patience. Guanxi is not the only driver of business negotiations in China but it is one of the skills you must develop to be successful. You have to approach your network building in a systematic and almost ritualistic way, understanding that guanxi places the same obligations on you as it does on your Chinese counterpart. Although you may think that the guanxi network is no different to business networking in the West, your Chinese counterpart will not think of it like that and will be quite offended if you suggest as much. The Chinese regard guanxi as unique to China. They regard it an integral part of negotiation and the performance of due diligence.

In imperial China and well into the era of communism, company profiles, third party testimonials, credit reports or audited financial reports did not exist. Guanxi networks and relationships were the only means to perform due diligence among Chinese business people. For the Westerner, this means that due diligence cannot be performed on your potential partner, or indeed on your own company, without being filtered through this uniquely Chinese system of reciprocal relationships and mutual obligation. In such a system, negotiations are continually ongoing and contracts are a last, and often worst line of defence for Western companies.

Saving and giving face

Maintaining balance and harmony is an important aspect of Chinese culture. Chinese do not want to lose face, and they also do not want to cause you to lose face. Therefore, they will rarely disagree with you in public and will instead emphasise friendly relations and cooperation. When you or your boss comes to town and both of you are treated with a great deal of respect and lavished with compliments, you may naturally assume that such a cooperative and friendly atmosphere will make your job negotiating a deal much easier. You will be pleasantly surprised by the comments and compliments of your Chinese counterparts, and you may soon believe that an agreement is well on the way.

However, quite often the opposite is true. In China, it's important not to be lulled into a false sense of complacency by this aspect of Chinese culture, and you should keep in perspective the compliments paid by your Chinese counterparts. Great effort must be made to understand the meanings behind the words and also the whole concept of giving, losing and saving face (see Chapter Four). There is a Chinese saying that loosely translated means, 'A person needs face like a tree needs bark'. In other words, face is more important that almost anything else and must be given, saved, enjoyed, considered or — in the Chinese worst case — lost.

On a superficial level, this means that the Chinese will look for a smooth outcome for most discussions — both for you and for them. However, you have to adjust your communication style to not expect too much from these initial meetings. What might appear to you as straightforward or even welcoming may not necessarily be so positive, especially if you show impatience, are over-direct, make loud complaints or condemn anyone. The Chinese, like many Asians, respect modesty and are not big talkers. They will expect you to listen more than you speak, to observe body language, to ask questions before you give an opinion, not to force anyone else to give an opinion, to show respect for hierarchy and age, and to pay attention to the personal and family concerns of your counterparts.

If you are not used to showing respect for the opinions of others and insist on doing business in your Western, decisive and highly individual way, you will not have much success negotiating in China. You must learn to use the essential differences in culture between the West and China as strength, not as an impediment.

Yes and no

Another aspect of the unwillingness to lose face is the Chinese reluctance to say a decisive 'yes' or 'no'. Not only do they not want to lose face, but they also don't want you to lose face by giving a direct answer that is not what you wanted to hear. The result is that you're never quite sure what's going on in a business meeting, presentation or negotiation, and you aren't allowed to ask because you won't get a straight answer. You might not get an answer at all.

Personal dignity or face is very important to the Chinese and this has particular relevance to decision-making. Face-saving tactics are often used in business to avoid giving a clear, logical response to proposals. This gives the Chinese side time to consider proposals and to wait until a personal relationship is further established. The negotiation itself will be slotted into the time-hallowed process of guanxi building and reciprocal obligations. Whatever was said or half-agreed at the initial meeting will be forgotten unless you made a clear note of what was agreed. Clearly, this oblique and largely instinctive behaviour is a way of buying time in negotiations and also of avoiding the disharmony created by giving straight yes/no replies to proposals or questions.

Chinese negotiating tactics

Other non-verbal techniques, such as vaguely worded and evasive questions and a love of paradox, are all part of the learning process for the Western business person in China. Those who are posted to China for a short time are rarely able to conquer these high-context and oblique negotiation processes. Many companies feel that the effort to invest in the necessary training is not worth it. However, to think in these terms is both shortsighted and negative. It is best to remember that a Chinese may well send you in the wrong direction if you ask for directions in the street simply not to lose face. I have personally experienced this in Shanghai and many other Chinese cities. For Western companies, a simple investment in preparation, research and intercultural training will help navigate the minefield of saving face in China.

Another way to succeed is to leave your ego at home. The Chinese pay attention to what you do, not what you say, so it's better to be understated and modest in all your actions and behavior. Show your Chinese counterparts respect and make an effort to get to know them on a more personal level. This will help you to gain their empathy for your position. Much is made of the elaborate banqueting, drinking and karaoke sessions in China. These might not seem like ideal negotiating forums, and indeed they are not, but they are an important way to bond with your Chinese counterparts and they should be respected for that alone.

Also, beware of thinking that absolutely no business goes on amid all the toasting and *gan-bei*s. You may not realise it, but these 'getting to know you' activities are not the prelude to negotiation. They are in some ways the opening of the play. You should be working out the script, just as the Chinese are, and getting ready to play your part in the unfolding drama.

I don't mean that you should be spouting endless business topics between drinking Chinese Mai Tai and eating Beijing Duck and singing 'My Way'. I mean that you should have a clear, strategic plan for what you want to get out of the relationship in the long run. You may be able to deliver this plan in a short message of thanks or a toast at the event itself. Whatever your vision is, you should be ready to enact it in slow and careful stages with the ultimate goal in mind.

Decision-making

When negotiating in China, remember that the entire procedure is a little like a team sport. In most companies, employees are team members for life. China itself is a huge national team that values cohesiveness and national identity above all.

It is important to pave the way for the first negotiation or presentation, to see your Chinese counterparts without a fixed agenda (that can be in your strategic plan). This process can take several months. Older Chinese can attend whole meetings without a substantive issue being discussed. Trust has to develop before bargaining begins. When negotiations finally occur, the Chinese do not necessarily pursue a win-win line, but rather one of fair play for those who have dealings with them.

They are particularly attracted to value-enhancing investors, such as those with expertise in accounting, marketing, technical systems and know-how. Ultimately, they tend to look for *good long-term relationships*. Once you reach the negotiating or presentation stage, be patient and listen. Bring along your own interpreter if legal or technical issues are to be discussed. Present written material in both English and Chinese, using simplified Chinese characters, and be very careful that translations are accurate. You will likely face a team of negotiators across the table. A key challenge will be to identify the real decision-maker in the group — there is usually only one — and the individual or individuals who can influence the decision-maker. Since established

Chinese companies are still hierarchical in nature, and Confucian in their respect systems, the final decision-maker may not even be in the room.

Always make an appointment and arrive on time. Face-to-face meetings are always preferred to other, more impersonal methods such as email. The most senior person in your team should be introduced first. It may appear that negotiations are proceeding very slowly but the main purpose of the first meeting is to get to know each other as the foundation for building a further relationship.

You should use your guanxi, or the relationships that you have developed with the local government, to develop support for your position. A capable Chinese team of your own can also help to bridge cultural differences and assist you in understanding the nuances of what is being said by your counterpart. A good team can also develop useful back channels with the other side that can smooth negotiations.

Remember that the Chinese negotiating process is set up to gather information and assist them in their learning curve. You will therefore have to be extremely careful about what you are offering in terms of technology exchange and intellectual property protection. Sometimes the guanxi system can shut down abruptly if it seems that you cannot offer this kind of value-added exchange or that you are no longer deemed useful. If you come into negotiations in China with a potential partner and simply hope to wing it, or to just learn the ropes from the partner without doing any other kind of due diligence, you are asking for trouble. There are potential 'bad partners' in China that are intent on stealing your intellectual property and technology right from the start. If you have a good local team and have prepared yourself carefully, you can quickly identify these bad partners as asset raiders and save yourself a lot of time and money.

Above all, be fair-minded, diplomatic and reasonable. If your Chinese counterpart believes that you are being unreasonable, they may not openly say so, but your negotiations are likely to stall and go nowhere. If you disagree with your counterpart, don't simply reject their position out of hand but carefully explain your reasoning. Trying to impose your own deadlines, threatening to abandon the negotiations, or indulging in displays of anger will undermine the sincerity of your position and cause irretrievable loss of face.

Contracts

The fact that China's legal system is underdeveloped and weakly enforced explains why relationships typically are valued more than laws in China. The value that Confucianism places on interpersonal obligations underlies this focus on relationships. Your Chinese counterparts will trust you to fulfil your end of a deal, not because you signed a binding contract but because *guanxi* obliges you to do so.

Since Chinese tend to negotiate the relationship and not the contract, it is quite common for contracts to be treated merely as first steps in the ongoing relationship. China's legal system is improving, but you may find that relevant laws, contracts, or tax policies are nothing more than a starting point in your negotiations.

The safest approach is to ensure that you know and trust your negotiating partner. Guanxi is essential for business negotiations, but maintaining an advantage can be difficult. Research shows that even among successful Western business people in China, post-signing renegotiation is the rule and not the exception. In general, Chinese business people feel that as long as the relationship is intact, negotiations should continue. In fact, negotiations are not supposed to end because that would mean the end of the relationship.

It is therefore essential for Westerners to expect that a post-contract negotiation will take place and to plan for this in advance in terms of allocating resources and appropriate time. They should also alert their own company headquarters, clients and partners to the probability that the contract signing is not the end of the process. This in turn means that Chinese counterparts should be vetted even more carefully at the beginning of the potential partnership, and difficult details should be explored early on in the negotiations.

The bottom line is that the agreement, if ever considered final, should be binding only in the sense that it is good for everyone involved and for the full realisation of the partnership's potential over time. The Chinese regard contracts as holistic (the value of the total relationship) rather than transactional. Western negotiators who try to enforce a transactional deal with a strict timetable are likely to end up with a 'contract' that is not worth the paper on which it is printed.

To manage risks well, conduct periodic guanxi audits to ensure that your negotiating team has maintained multiple ties with the other side. If your guanxi comes from just one person, your deal could collapse if he or she quits. Moreover, because your guanxi as an outsider may be no match for a better offer from an insider, be sure to develop your best alternative to a negotiated agreement. Finally, don't forget that guanxi cuts both ways — your business partner will expect you to return any favours granted.

Action points

1. What do you understand by the idea that the Chinese negotiate the relationship not the contract? What are the significant differences you foresee or have experienced between the Chinese style of negotiating and the style you are used to?

2. 'A person needs face like a tree needs bark.' List out the principal ways in which the concept behind this Chinese proverb is likely to influence your negotiations and business dealings in China.

3. Consider how you are going to build a guanxi network into your overall negotiating plan. Who will be on your Chinese team? Who will be your translator and interpreter? Who will be your preferred partner?

4. Actively seek out and take advice from experienced expats/consultants and local Chinese in the market or markets you choose, so that you are fully prepared for market entry and business development through successful negotiations (of the relationship).

CHAPTER SEVEN

GOVERNANCE AND ETHICS

THE BUSINESS LANDSCAPE IN CHINA is complex and difficult to understand at first sight. The most obvious difference from Western countries is the much larger role that government plays in business in China. Foreign enterprises may well find that several agencies have regulatory authority over them or impose demanding reporting requirements. The demands of one agency may conflict with the demands of another.

If you want to succeed in China, you must temporarily forget how business is done in your own country and focus entirely on China. Although Chinese commercial law is increasingly clear and complete, some laws are weakly enforced and others are fitfully applied. Courts can interpret the law very differently from one city or province to another. In a dispute between a foreign and a Chinese firm, you may find that a court is impartial but that would be the exception. In other words, you need a highly prepared team of legal specialists to deal with problems as they arise.

A key element of any China strategy is to have a thoroughly prepared and fully advised plan to protect intellectual property (IP). Your team needs to be extremely prepared on IP issues as they relate to China and you will need to work with IP attorneys and specialists who have hands-on experience, especially if proprietary technology is essential to your business.

China changes too fast for one person to keep up with all of the regulatory and legal issues impacting your China business. You will need core team members who have a feel for how government and regulatory regimes function in China and capable local staff to provide support. Some foreign firms complain that the playing field in China is not level. Enforcement of regulatory measures often targets foreign invested enterprises while ignoring violations by domestic companies. Chinese media is quick to jump on mistakes made by a foreign company, often without listening to the company's side of the story. To avoid being damaged your team needs expatriates and experienced consultants who understand Chinese business culture and how the building of strong relationships can protect your operations.

Confucian values

There is a common myth among Westerners that all Asian countries share the same 'Asian values', attitudes and approach to business. In past decades Asian politicians like Lee Kuan Yew, the father of Singapore, or Dr. Mahathir of Malaysia have supported this myth by drawing attention to the 'decadence' of Western individualism and by declaring that the economic strength of their countries is due to a strong collectivist culture based on Confucian family values (derived from China) such as order, respect, hierarchy and harmony.

'Too much democracy' is cited as the reason for social instability in the West, freedom of speech as the generator of cultural weakness, unfettered individualism as the cause of the breakdown of group and family consciousness. These stereotypes have taken root in the way that Westerners think about Chinese business and culture. To a certain extent they have some basis in reality but they are by no means the whole truth. They obscure significant differences of culture among, say, China, Japan, Thailand and the Philippines.

It is true that participatory democracy is almost entirely absent in China. It is also true that the emphasis on group and family collectivism, authority and hierarchy, respect and paternalism have led to serious distortions of business ethics in the country such as government and local government corruption, the encouragement of cronyism, favoured treatment for financial loans and family nepotism.

But corruption exists to a certain extent in all societies. The revelations since 2008 of what has transpired in the financial markets of the West suggest that the more individualist West's tendency to allow workers greater freedom to operate on their own has encouraged a widespread culture of insider trading, manipulation of markets and inter-bank collusion.

Whatever their relative merits or drawbacks, Chinese Confucian values have proved extremely beneficial for building the foundations of the country's prosperity, especially when competent economists and technocrats (many of them educated in the West) have been allowed to guide team-conscious and highly trained people. Confucian values could be said to have fostered high savings rates and hence substantial capital for economic growth. The average savings rate in China is around 50 per cent as a percentage of income, one of the highest in the world.

The Chinese passion for education has produced an almost unlimited supply of educated labour and high-quality engineers. In addition, the stricter regime imposed by society and schools, as well as compulsory military service, have produced disciplined workers who respond well to clearly defined routines and working in a team.

It is easy to forget that the dynamic Chinese economy that we see today, particularly in the eastern and southern coastal cities, has in fact become successful only in relatively recent times. Even though China's socialist market economy became the second largest economy in the world in 2010, the market-oriented reforms that were instigated by Deng Xiaoping only really took off in the 1990s. Given such rapid progress, it is perhaps no surprise that China has still not managed to close the enormous gap between the privileged few and the vast majority of the population.

Even now, when you might expect the Chinese to take their foot off the accelerator just a little, they continue to work as if they were still poor. This attitude has some basis in reality. Even though China is on the edge of becoming the largest economy in the world, China's GDP per capita is still around $6,000 while that of the US is $50,000 and that of the UK is $40,000. Nevertheless, Western business executives working in Asia would do well to recognise the strengths of the Chinese model, particularly its extremely high work ethic, and to consider how the strengths could become the backbone for economic success in their own countries.

Family ownership and succession

The downside of Confucian values derives from the attitude that the interests of family and close friends must be protected at all costs and placed before the public interest. 'Family' can be interpreted to include the inner circle or loyal subordinates or even government officers. The relationship of trust that these 'family' members have developed means that major transactions are sometimes executed without legal due diligence and the usual commercial procedures.

This tradition derives from the 'gentlemen's agreements' prevalent in Chinese business circles in the past and that still characterise the approach to contracts and decisions in China today. Although some deference is paid to legal and corporate governance requirements, the overwhelming factor determining the outcome of business negotiations in China is usually trust and the length of the relationship. It is therefore essential to have a clear understanding of the nuances of Chinese social and business culture before entering into negotiations with a Chinese partner or beginning business operations in China.

One of the most pervasive aspects of Chinese business culture is the determination of founding families to retain control. The contrast with Western business cultures based on the Anglo-Saxon model, where shareholder value is paramount, is marked.

The function of the firm in the private sector in China is primarily to generate family wealth. Most of China's new class of billionaires come from profitable family-owned businesses. The firms exist to provide shareholder value only for people at the very top, which is why many large Chinese companies are governed more hierarchically than their Western counterparts. Such patronage systems reinforce feelings of mutual dependency, obligation, loyalty and trust. Gifts made by a patron are unstated and not immediately reciprocated but such favours can be called in at a later date. A patronage relationship can last a lifetime. Personal connections are therefore vital to getting things done.

China has more than ten million private companies that account for about 60 per cent of GDP. According to the All-China Federation of Industry and Commerce, more than 80 per cent of private firms can be classified as family businesses. Their significance to China's economy is therefore enormous, and so too is the importance of handing over the family business from one generation to another.

Succession is a pressing issue in China not only because many family businesses are so young — many enterprises were born during the economic reforms of the 1980s — but also because various thorny issues have been thrown up by the lack of succession plans and uncertainty over the process. One of the main concerns of Chinese family bosses is the lack of professional management because there's no mature market for professional managers and no proper incentive system to recruit, promote and compensate them. Another concern is the emphasis on male succession when the single male heir (due to China's one-child policy) has no interest in carrying on the business.

One of the ironies of China's astonishing leap into modernity is that it has been largely driven by the family firm, founded by men who are imbued with traditional Confucian precepts of filial duty, harmony and clearly defined gender roles. This has left many female members of China's business dynasties torn between family duty and the potential of an independent career. Many are proud graduates of the world's most prestigious universities and business schools and feel limited by a glass ceiling of tradition.

However, the traditional model of splitting the business between the male heirs is beginning to look increasingly old-fashioned. A growing number of China's patriarchs are coming to the conclusion that slavishly following tradition will not only stifle women's personal and professional development, it will also pose a significant challenge to the sustainability of the family enterprise. They are increasingly turning to trusts, holding companies and family offices as mechanisms to transfer assets to the next generation while retaining the skills of highly capable women and preserving the efficiencies of the bigger entity. Many women already play a role in managing the family's existing financial and real estate assets, making it a natural progression to move to a more formal position as director or CEO of a family umbrella company. This trend is likely to gain momentum in the future.

Corporate governance

Among the reasons that family businesses in China seek to retain control is that costs of internal auditing and reporting are thereby lowered, succession issues and compensation systems are more comfortably handled, and companies can be treated as personal fiefdoms. Although much stronger corporate governance regimes have been established in international financial centres with developed capital markets such as Hong Kong and Singapore, it is true that a widening gap remains between laws and implementation in China.

A more dynamic regulatory environment, together with the increasing complexity of business transactions and significant advances in information technology, has resulted in an upgrade of the corporate governance framework in various Asian countries. However, corporate social responsibility (CSR) and protection of the environment do not feature strongly in the corporate reputation agenda of many Chinese executives. A recent survey of six southern Chinese cities found that environmental awareness was strong amongst managers and local government officials but implementation was hampered by the fear of sacrificing economic growth. I recently interviewed the chairman of a family-owned Chinese firm who said he knew nothing of environmental matters ('I leave that to HR') and very little about CSR issues. However, as chairman and CEO combined, he was aware of succession issues and was considering splitting the roles 'sometime in the future'.

To date, the corporate governance framework in China has been weak owing to the legacy of a planned economy with substantial Party interference in the running of state-owned enterprises (SOEs). Despite much talk of reform, SOEs are still the backbone of China's economy, producing over 50 per cent of the nation's goods and services, and employing over half of China's workers. The lack of accountability and transparency in SOEs has contributed to the problem of corruption and bribery in China. However, change is taking place, largely driven by the opening up of the markets to the international economy and the desire to attract foreign investment.

Reform has generally drawn on continental European trends, with the institution of a supervisory board as well as Anglo-Saxon models. Important changes have also recently taken place in the corporate governance of SOEs. Reforms have been concentrated mainly in the areas of the ownership function and the legal and regulatory framework for SOEs, and the introduction of a set of performance assessment measures for SOE board members and managers. Enforcement of corporate governance regulations also appears to be improving. These are positive indications that the Chinese authorities are at least aware of the problem, although there is till a great deal to be done to reduce the number of SOEs and improve their governance.

Corruption

Corruption exists in all societies, not least in the financial markets of the West. In China, patronage systems and collectivism have inevitably encouraged corruption in one form or another, which has flourished according to the relative strength or weakness of the rule of law. However, Western businesses should also be aware that ethical problems in doing business in China or perceptions of such are often traceable to misunderstandings and lack of cultural awareness. A careful study of Chinese culture should precede your business forays into China.

In dealing with Chinese companies, remember that the Chinese educational system still uses a certain amount of shaming and this naturally results in people who have a great aversion to being embarrassed. The issue of giving face, well known in the West, recognises this sensitivity. When you are faced with a clear reluctance to address a problem despite repeated attempts, or encounter dubious attempts to explain a problem away, the person is usually embarrassed. Often a personal visit and respectful probing one on one — possibly in a relaxed social situation — can be a better way to solve the problem. Show respect by bringing solutions with you. Learn how to be firm in a way that shows personal and cultural respect.

A lie is not always frowned upon in Chinese culture. Chinese culture will accept a 'white lie', especially when respect or face is involved. This concept can be a little difficult for Westerners to understand so don't be too ready to criticise. Often a white lie is used to either avoid embarrassing or damaging someone, saying something that they think will disrespect you, or saying something they think will undermine your authority. Do not become aggressive because of this, but rather be grateful for this form of respect. You should practise solving these kinds of problems with discretion and diplomacy.

The concept of guanxi and the obligations it carries have been discussed in Chapter Five, but personal friendship can be stronger than guanxi. Sometimes various obligations will collide, and a Chinese person will spend considerable time working out a solution that gives respect to all parties, often avoiding the literal truth in the process. When doing high-level business in China a smart business person should learn to recognise such shades of grey and develop strategies accordingly, as Chinese people are inherently skilled at seeking out the solution to the problem.

Although legal protection has generally been weak, one of the most effective anti-corruption factors for private sector firms in China is the sharing of prospective high profits. This prospect aligns the interests of government officials with those of entrepreneurs and investors, thereby ensuring that all parties fulfil their roles and protect the firm's reputation to make the enterprise successful.

Generally speaking, Asian executives rate corruption well below inflation and inadequate infrastructure or labour regulations as an obstacle to doing business. In part this is because Western law has not been central to Asian experience except in cities like Hong Kong and Singapore that were under colonial rule for a long time.

China, by contrast is said not to have rule of law but rule *by* law. A successful entrepreneur or a government official will command a large project to be done and it will be done. His power may be theoretically limited by the need for permits, but he will order his lawyers to find a law that allows what he wants, or he will even get a new law passed. Anyone who wants to do business in China should be aware of the variety of legal systems in operation, and of their relative strengths and weaknesses.

In such a huge economy, people are always wary of new, unknown customers. Building trust and an inclusive relationship will involve time and often some financial investment as well. When mutual trust deepens, so also can a sense of mutual openness and fairness. But for every barrel of apples there are usually a couple of bad ones so if you encounter consistent problems with ethics, change companies or partners.

Act carefully and sensibly. Have your designs registered in China and let the source company know you have done this. Design sensible contracts and protect your intellectual property carefully. Specify the parameters of a copy in the contract to avoid later arguments and litigation. Often you will flush out dishonest players when you ask them to sign a contract, even if the contract is merely a negotiating ploy on the route to a long-term relationship.

Whether hiring staff, investing in a joint venture or appointing a local distributor, carrying out due diligence is indispensable when launching a business in and with China for the first time. The key objective of due diligence is to verify the trustworthiness of partners and employees, and to discover any of those bad apples in the barrel before proceeding with any significant investment. Nowadays there are numerous legal and risk assessment specialists with offices in China that provide business intelligence, background checks and risk assessment consultancy. However, no amount of due diligence will protect a foreign investor from a collapse in business relations. It is vital that any market entry with Chinese partners at home and abroad is based on trust above all. Every effort must be made to ensure that a strategic partner is trusted.

Business gifts and gift-giving

Many Western business people new to China are advised of the importance of gift-giving to Chinese culture, business or otherwise. But why is this so important to Chinese people? And how is giving a gift different to corruption or bribery?

As we have seen, China's culture is steeped in Confucianism, which is based largely on respect, relationships and rituals with the intent of maintaining social and family harmony. To maintain their relationships with their family, friends and co-workers, Chinese feel the need to demonstrate their care and respect. This can take the form of giving a gift when invited to someone's house or company, as well as picking up the bill when dining with friends. Additionally, outside of one's immediate circle of friends and family, this practice is also used as a way of requesting or giving thanks for favours done.

Giving a gift also has a strong connection with giving someone face. When dining with friends or business contacts, the act of picking up the bill allows a person to demonstrate their respect and enthusiasm. This not only creates face, but also acts to strengthen the relationship between the two or more parties.

There is a key difference between this type of gift-giving and the traditional bribe. The goal of a regular gift is to demonstrate your respect for an individual and your commitment to creating or maintaining a relationship with them. Giving the gift will not show that a deal has been struck. However, not presenting a gift may make you appear impolite and uncultured. In contrast, a bribe in China is often a specific sum of hard currency within a red envelope.

Other common forms of bribery within China take the form of company stock, cuts of profits, and expensive gifts, such as cars, luxury watches and high-end electronics. In the case of an actual bribe, an individual may demand (directly or indirectly) that something be given in order to ensure a certain outcome. However, the exact difference between a gift and a bribe can remain unclear within the rather oblique Chinese business environment, and it is not uncommon for companies to set limits on the value of gifts that can be given or received.

There is also the potential for the concepts of gift-giving to cause worry and stress for the Chinese themselves and even damage relationships. This is because of the tradition of guanxi and obligation. When someone is treated to dinner, it is expected that the kindness will be returned at some point in the future. When a Chinese couple receives a gift from a friend for their child, not only will they feel compelled to buy a gift for their friend's child, but they will also take care to give a gift of at least an equal value to the one received. If a business client feels that they have not received an appropriate gift, or if no gift is given, then this has the potential to damage the relationship.

For the Westerner doing business in China, while it is not necessary to observe these practices as strictly as the local Chinese, it is recommended to pay more attention to close Chinese friends, important business contacts, and anyone within the government bureaucracy who has the power to make your life or business difficult. Remember, giving a gift it not always a bribe. Often it is a method for building and maintaining a strong and mutually beneficial relationship.

Sometimes, due to the official policy tightening the rules on gift-giving, there may be times when a gift will not be accepted. Should you find yourself in this situation, graciously say you understand and withdraw the gift. Smaller, less expensive items will not be seen as a bribe. The Chinese do not usually accept a gift, invitation or favour when it is first presented, but will politely refuse two or three times to reflect modesty and humility. Accepting something in haste makes a person look aggressive and greedy, as does opening it in front of the giver.

When or if a gift is given, it should be offered with two hands. Any gift offered with two hands should always be received with two hands. It's traditional to bring a gift when invited to someone's home. Fresh flowers or fruit are recommended, and it is a good idea to bring eight, rather than the typical Western dozen. Eight is a lucky number. The more expensive the gift, the more respectful, but don't go over the top or you will embarrass your hosts, who may feel the need to go out of their way to return your generosity.

Be sure to be fair with your gift-giving: don't give something better to the secretary in the office than to the wife of your Chinese partner, and don't give gifts to one group of employees and not another — they will soon know. Often, it's better to give something that can be shared, like cookies or chocolate. Never give a clock as a gift. Traditional superstitions regard this as counting the seconds to the recipient's death. Also avoid giving fans. The word for fan in Chinese is related to the expression for splitting up. Never give a man a green hat. The Chinese expression 'wearing a green hat' means that someone's wife is unfaithful.

Gifts from your own country are always welcome and very much appreciated. Don't wrap any gifts from home before arriving in China, as they may be unwrapped in Customs. If possible, have your gifts wrapped in red paper, which is considered a lucky colour. Pink, gold and silver are also acceptable colours for gift-wrap. Gifts wrapped in yellow paper with black writing are given only to the dead. Also, check on the regional variations of colour meanings — a safe colour in Beijing could get you in trouble in Shenzhen. Your safest option is to entrust the task of gift-wrapping to a store or hotel that offers this service.

Most Chinese I have dealt with are kind and sensitive with a great desire to learn and better themselves. They also generally show great respect to foreigners. Return that respect by working *with* them and never treat them as servants. Help them to achieve your mutually beneficial goals. Show integrity in your dealings and it is more often than not reciprocated. The ability to form strong friendships despite difficulties is a very satisfying aspect of cross-cultural business dealings, and it is these relationships that will ultimately form the strongest future ethical platform.

Action points

1. List out the Chinese values you most admire and consider whether they are equally to be found in Western countries. For example, could they become drivers of economic success in your own country or are they already in operation there in some form? If so, what makes these values so successful in China while your own more 'developed' country seems to be lagging behind?

2. Consider the weakness or relative strength of regulatory systems, the rule of law and corporate

governance regimes in China, and how this may or may not affect your business strategies.

3. Name what you regard as the top drivers of Chinese consumer and social behaviour, and ask yourself whether these trends play a significant part in your business expansion plans.

4. Make a clear list with two columns of the ways a gift may be given legally and illegally in business situations in China. Take both legal and local Chinese advice from trusted sources as to how to deal with the potential pitfalls of gift-giving in China, the customs, short-cut temptations, examples and experiences of Western companies.

5. Prepare a strategic plan to ensure you choose highly intelligent, well educated and strongly motivated Chinese partners and that members of your local team are a well-balanced mix of experienced expatriates and local Chinese. Take advice from them on all cultural, political, legal and social matters that may impact your business.

CHAPTER EIGHT

BUILDING THE LEADERSHIP SKILLS FOR CHINA

NOW THAT WE HAVE CONSIDERED how to develop confidence through learning about the business culture and etiquette of China as a whole, and of individual regions in particular, it is time to address the question of performance. How will you perform within these markets? How will you gain credibility and trust with the knowledge you have acquired? How will you communicate and show leadership so that you can develop your business skills once you have overcome the initial and subsequent entry barriers?

The remarkable economic growth of China in recent decades is undoubtedly one of the most significant developments in world history. The rebalancing of global economic power towards the East continues today while Europe struggles with the aftermath of the sovereign debt crisis and America with the fallout from years of high spending and low saving.

As far as we can see into the future, the high GDP growth rates, high savings ratios and increasing affluence of the developed and developing regions and cities of China will attract more and more Western companies to invest in the Chinese renaissance, develop pan-China operations and attempt to marry their business and leadership practices with those of China.

The big question is whether those attempting to enter the China market for the first time have the leadership skills that are required. Are there any significant differences, for example, between the leadership styles of Chinese executives and those that you are familiar with in the West? Or are they simply the result of Chinese companies operating in a different culture or at a less mature stage of corporate development?

Leadership at its best is transformational. It means having a vision of the future, a strategy to reach that mission, and the ability to inspire others to reach that goal. With the widespread adoption of the MBA standard in management education throughout the world, and the rapid transfer of management techniques through the web and international business schools, this style of leadership and its ability to transform does not differentiate the West from the East. It differentiates mediocre companies from highly successful companies all over the world.

Cultural differences

As has been shown in Chapter Two, cultural differences between the Chinese and Western economies are often a question of emphasis. For example, there are still enterprises led by family patriarchs in Western countries but they are not as common as they are in China. There are founders' descendants at the helm of some of America's and Europe's largest public and private companies, just as there are family dynasties heading up conglomerates in Beijing, Shanghai and Hong Kong. However, there are many more of them in China and in this sense there are some important differences in leadership style between China and the West.

Professional senior managers and not family members run most Western companies. Well-managed companies have programmes for developing leaders and sophisticated succession plans. Many future leaders rise to the top through such internal programmes, although as we have seen in recent times this is not always the case. Some top executives in Western companies are parachuted into highly competitive sectors, such as investment banking, on mouth-watering compensation and bonus packages.

However, Western companies are usually reliant on capital markets for their equity and debt capital (rather than directly or indirectly on government or on family wealth) and so their leaders pay more attention to stock markets than their counterparts in China. These stock markets tend to impose strict regulations about executive behaviour, performance and succession.

This situation is gradually changing as the Chinese government tightens regulatory regimes and corporate governance requirements, but again generally speaking, there is less freedom of action for executives and boards in the West than in China. It may be that Chinese family firms will eventually follow the evolutionary path of Western companies towards professional management and capital obtained almost entirely from the capital markets. Several Asian countries, such as Japan, are showing progress in this direction. In the meantime, Chinese companies' political and family connections continue to play a role that is far less evident or common in the West, and this is even truer of the large number of state-owned enterprises (SOEs) that produce almost half of the country's goods and services.

Leadership styles

The leadership styles evident in China are also less varied than in the West. The authoritarian leader who gives out the firm's direction by fiat is more common in the China, whereas the leader who relies on teamwork and participation is common in both the West and in some Asian countries like Japan. The leader who empowers and delegates to others, particularly large semi-autonomous divisions, is gradually becoming more evident in China but this leadership style is far more common in Western companies. Overall, adaptability is less common and less valued in China than in the West.

These are important points to bear in mind. But as you develop your business in China, this apparent conservatism should not discourage you. Information technology and the internet are bringing out a type of leadership that is becoming rapidly more evident in China: entrepreneurial, innovative and ambitious.

Take Dr Victor Fung of Li & Fung, a traditional Chinese family-owned trading company based in Hong Kong. Victor Fung was educated at Harvard University. He also works within the close-knit Chinese world of relationships. His company uses technology to obtain maximum efficiency from the global supply chain, handling every stage of the process from raw material to manufacturing high-demand consumer goods at a much lower cost than in the West. In many ways Victor Fung is an old-style Chinese taipan. But he is also a sophisticated, Western-style technocrat capable of communicating his leadership style and business techniques to a global audience. As such he represents the new style of Chinese leader. The question is whether this type of leadership will eventually become the principal or even the only one in China.

Clearly, Chinese companies will gradually come to rely more on professional employees and professional services than they do today. In the process, it is likely that a less autocratic and more participative style of leadership will emerge to resemble that of the West. Certainly the younger Chinese of Generation Y are voting with their feet to move to companies where this style of leadership is more in evidence, along with an entrepreneurial spirit and focus on innovation. Even so, significant cultural differences will remain.

Communicating across cultures

For this reason, every newcomer to the Chinese business world must learn the art of cross-cultural communication and intercultural intelligence. As we have seen, in China's high-context business culture, where mutual trust and understanding are the essential pre-requisites to building successful partnerships, much emphasis is placed on respectful behaviour, awareness of position and knowledge of local customs.

For the Western business person used to selling products and services through tightly focused presentations or in direct negotiations that have clear goals and outcomes, communication is based largely on the lingua franca of English wherever they are in the world. The message in English is usually expressed in bullet points, PowerPoint slides, videos and factual material provided by sales and marketing, finance or other relevant departments. In larger companies, a Western CEO or chairman may give the occasional speech in English at prestigious local seminars, openings and launches, as well as at international conferences in order to maintain and develop the company's reputation and brand.

However, in China the cultural context of the speech or presentation is just as important as is knowledge of local etiquette and customs when attending a business dinner. It is true that the business lingua franca of China is becoming increasingly English (I gave a speech in English to Chinese students in Shanghai recently), particularly in the first-tier coastal cities, and cross-cultural email communication is often in English. But a one-size-fits-all English presentation for China is unlikely to succeed. Every presentation must be coloured by local references, by knowledge of local customs, and by sensitivity to the local business culture.

As a speechwriter, I learned never to write exactly the same speech or presentation to be given in Tokyo or Kuala Lumpur, Seoul or Singapore. The same is true of

China and its vastly different cities and provinces. The local context not only adds flavour to a speech, but it also determines whether the speech is successful or not. A Westerner giving a presentation in Malaysia should be reasonably informed about Islam, have some knowledge of the ethnic mix of Malays and Chinese in Malaysia, and might be aware that Sharia law has influenced the marketing of certain products in the Malaysian market. A Westerner speaking in Beijing or Guangzhou should be aware of the importance of Chinese New Year or of the colour red for prosperity or the lucky number eight, which the Chinese try to include in their phone numbers, passports and addresses.

These are very simple examples. In many ways it doesn't matter so much *what* Westerners know about local culture. It is important that they show they know *something*. For that something will give them an entrée to the business circles they are attempting to penetrate.

There was an ancient historical perspective that the Chinese nation was superior to others, and occasionally you might find echoes of this still resonating in certain less-developed areas of modern China. Due to this and other factors, Chinese culture has a strong collective but also a local aspect. Indeed, as in the West, national, family or friendship ties are still superior to any other kind of relationship. This concept gives great strength to being in the inner circle. Western business people must steadily focus on entering inner circles by tailoring their communications more and emphasising fairness and mutual goals.

Local languages

Some knowledge of Mandarin ('high' Chinese) or even Hokkien (Fujian province) or Cantonese (Hong Kong and Guangdong province) is also important. In an era of 24/7 global communications, of texting and social media, it would be easy to assume that the English language united the people of the world and that is all that a Western business executive needs. However, in China the opposite is true: English is the second language, a language used in business only when interfacing with foreigners, while the national language and a host of accompanying dialects are the predominant means of communication.

It is remarkable when travelling in Asian countries how readily smiles appear and doors open when a Westerner speaks a phrase in Thai or Korean, Chinese or Japanese. Often it is enough to know the words for 'good morning' and 'good evening' or 'how are you/fine thank you' in the local language for an extra level of respect and warmth to be added to the relationship.

If this is true while travelling, imagine how much more valuable those few words are in the context of a business dinner in China, a home invitation or when added to speeches, presentations and internal communications. Unless you are a polymath, it is not necessary to learn Mandarin in any depth. Your representative or members of your team can communicate for you when fluency is required. But an occasional phrase (perhaps just two words) or knowledge of a local expression dropped into a text can generate that essential rapport between audience and speaker that make a sales presentation or a keynote speech equally memorable.

How am I perceived?

In high-context cultures, perception is as important, perhaps even more important than what is said. If the way you communicate comes over as lecturing or careless of where you are or whom you are talking to (the one-size-fits-all syndrome), your audience will not warm to you. If on the other hand you show awareness of the cultural diversity or ethnic backgrounds of your audience, you will gain respect and support for the message you are aiming to convey.

Remember that your Chinese audience may well be formulating responses to you or your message in the silences and pauses in your presentation, even when being asked a question, rather than in the more obviously amusing or applause-worthy sections. So be prepared to be scrutinised and adapt your words, your timing, and your body language accordingly. Don't run around the stage or over-compensate with lots of gestures. Be cool, take stock, and allow a pause for a 'foreign' or unusual thought to be registered.

All cultures are different, and Chinese culture is no exception. So try to allow a moment for your message or your joke to be mentally translated and digested, even when it's accompanied (as it should be) with the occasional local reference to make it more palatable. Above all, remember that the Chinese have their own first language and will need clarity of enunciation, as well as clear, simple and brief messages in English to absorb whatever you want to say.

The Chinese are great storytellers, so go ahead and tell a good story with the time-hallowed 'beginning, middle and end' structure. Announce what you want to say (a clear and unique message), develop that message with any qualifications and challenges and cross-currents you consider necessary, and return to the main message. Or to put it another way: announce what you're going to say, say it, and tell them that you've said it. Finish off with some memorable uplift and/or phrase. And if you really want to ensure that you get through, use the very latest technology in all your presentations.

Many Chinese are now technology geeks to the hilt, and they possess the very latest in smartphone, PDA, videoconferencing and voice interactive tools and gadgets. They are fanatical about the latest technology, so make sure you don't roll out the old PowerPoint slides with an overhead projector and a faulty microphone.

Building successful cross-cultural teams

Successful cross-cultural communications build successful cross-cultural teams. Sensitive political, social or religious issues that have the potential to offend your counterparts or hosts or other members of the local team you have assembled should be avoided. Unifying cultural experiences, such as a shared sense of humour and a belief in the value of teamwork and cohesiveness, should be highlighted.

Generally speaking, you should try to implement the principle of diversity and inclusiveness in the way you do business in China. As ambassadors both for your companies and for the countries where you originate, you should show cultural sensitivity as soon as you arrive and try to develop a network of trusted business associates and a local team that reflects the country's or region's local diversity.

In some provinces or cities you will find yourself dealing with more than one ethnic group as well as expatriates. You will have to find a way of showing sensitivity to the needs of each of these groups. A strong team spirit and work ethic can be developed from such different elements, as well as enduring relationships with the local business network. Westerners who are able to build a reputation of being fair-minded and inclusive will usually succeed in winning people over in China, whereas those with a manipulative or authoritarian or condescending style will damage mutual trust.

To succeed in China, you must have a team that understands China's business culture and can work successfully within that culture. Your business in China will depend on the ability of your team to develop effective guanxi relationships with Chinese partners, colleagues and employees. It is essential you find the right people with good working knowledge of the Chinese market and regulatory environment for your business or industry. These people will have to find domestic information sources that related directly to your business plans.

It is not necessary that everybody on your team speaks Chinese, but having some Chinese speakers will definitely benefit you. Many subtleties and nuances of expression can be lost in translation, even if the interpreter is world-class. You will receive a much broader and more immediate understanding of local business issues and conditions if you have Chinese speakers in your team.

Some companies believe a strong expatriate presence in China is essential for success. Others send a minimum of expatriates to get their China operations up and running. They then try to localise the team as quickly as possible. Whatever strategy you choose, you should have a China leadership team that consists of some expatriates, local support staff for these expatriates, and people from your home headquarters to lead and support the China team. This is necessary to avoid misunderstanding and poor communication between the China team and your home base.

The headquarters back-up team needs a basic understanding of how business in China works. They do not have to be specialists, but they should be careful not to immediately blame the China team if business is initially difficult. The expatriates should also remember that the headquarters team is often dealing with a number of issues that are unrelated to China.

Many companies cannot afford an in-house China specialist. Entrepreneurs and small and medium enterprises (SMEs) are likely to rely heavily on experienced China lawyers, accountants, due diligence consultants and other experts to develop their China business. However, all companies should have some form of in-house China expertise. Teams should be trained through executive coaching and high-level courses to understand China business in depth as well as the overall business/cultural environment in the Asia Pacific.

Action points

1. Jot down what you consider your own leadership style or way of doing things, and then compare this with any experience you have had of Chinese companies. Are there any significant differences, or is it simply a matter of emphasis and perception?

2. Imagine that you have to give a speech or presentation about your business in three Chinese cities (large, medium and small). Write down what you might add to the speech to give it a little more local colour, or to get the largely local audience on your side. Try to choose cities that are known for being quite different.

3. Consider what are the most sensitive issues in the Chinese market(s) where you operate and how you might avoid them or show you that you recognise them in the way that you build your teams, choose partners and show leadership.

4. Write down what you see as the driving values of the local Chinese culture and map out how you could incorporate them into a speech or presentation about your company, brand or product.

CONCLUSION

THE ROAD MAP TO GREATER SUCCESS

THE ROAD TO DOING BUSINESS in China is challenging but it is undoubtedly worth the effort. If you want to grow your confidence, your business and your brand in China you should follow the advice set out in this book, developing your knowledge and mind-set as you go along. That is the Chinese way of doing things. If you can learn to listen and not assert yourself continually, to observe and accept traditions and behaviours that may often seem oblique and even time wasting, to be patient and not expect immediate rewards, you will be on your way to becoming an accepted, long-term partner in the Chinese business world.

Whether you are a business owner, entrepreneur, JV partner, new subsidiary of a Western company, or the largest of multinationals, the only way to unlock Chinese markets is by taking the kind of strategic approach outlined in this book. This book is not the end of the learning process. It is the beginning of a long and fruitful journey towards business success in China.

As outlined in Chapter Three, each province and city in the country has its own traditions as well as its own economic dynamics and requires a different focus. Once you have mentally conquered the chapters of this book, you will have the required knowledge to put your knowledge into action and to tackle the subtleties of business and social behaviour that are unique to your market and sector in China. But to really develop your business, you will have to go further. You will have to deepen that knowledge.

There is no short cut to business success in China. You will need to *immerse* yourself in the history, business customs and culture of the country in order to expand or build a permanent presence. This immersion is not achievable in a day, or a week, but requires constant attention and a genuine interest, indeed passion. I recently heard a senior trade official from the West say on return from China, 'you have to go back to being a child: inquisitive, curious, watching and learning, play-acting and role-playing.' That's exactly the mind-set.

The sooner you can drop local topics, religious festivals or contemporary topics into your business conversation, for example, the sooner that all-important trust will be built. Politics is the exception to this rule. Don't get involved in any political discussion or comments about the government (you don't always know who is at your table or the next). On the other hand, be ready to enter with relish into the daily life, customs, religious and family festivals, business entertaining, and all the other aspects of the local culture of the province or city in which you are operating or intend to operate.

Remember the essential '4 Ps' of doing business in China, and remind yourself of their importance every day:

- **P**atience: Remember that credibility and trust are key in China and they cannot be built overnight or even in a couple of years.

- **P**resence: Be there on a regular basis, always contactable in person, the face and the presence of your company.

- **P**resentation: Tailor your behaviour, communications and personal branding to your Chinese audience.

- **P**erspective: Look at things from the viewpoint of someone with another background, in a different business, social and religious culture to your own.

Consideration and respect should be at the heart of everything you do, and remember that small gestures can often be as important as large ones. Observe how local Chinese business people behave, what they wear, how they greet one another, how they eat. If you follow their example, you will build business relationships and friendships that last a lifetime.

Business travel and cultural resources

Nowadays, there are plenty of business books on China, but many of them are academic and conceptual. Some of them are hard going. Many focus almost entirely on business management styles or legal, tax and regulatory issues as a preparation for entering the market. These are obviously important issues and will need to be studied by you and your local team or consultant at the very earliest stage. However, in addition to these essential 'hardware' guides, cultural 'software' in the form of a good contemporary travel book (preferably full of personal experience), and some books on how best to travel in and enjoy China are recommended.

An introduction to the language, with some simple phrases, is also useful even if you are largely employing local people. If you can say *Ni hau?* ('Hello' in Mandarin) or *Gay ho ma?* ('How are you?' in Cantonese), your company is already on the road to being accepted. In intensively Buddhist or Muslim parts of the country, some knowledge of religious beliefs is also required, if only to say that you have visited a temple or mosque and been favourably impressed — you even remembered to take off your shoes at the required place!

Many business people come to China with a readiness to learn, but just as many (and perhaps more) come with a mind-set that is still firmly rooted in their own countries in what is loosely called 'the West'. North Americans, Europeans, Australians and New Zealanders often find in the province or city of China where they are posted, or where they are attempting to set up and expand their business, a ready-made expatriate world (often a defined area of living and relaxing and entertaining) where their Western habits of thought and behaviour are supported and encouraged.

Many of those employed by multinational companies never attempt to step outside this world into the local culture, or bother to find out what makes their Chinese work colleagues or business partners and prospects tick. Some stick fondly to the belief that Western ways of doing things are somehow superior to the etiquette, beliefs and traditions of Chinese culture.

This attitude is easily supported by the ubiquity of the internet, social media and spoken English. However, although this modus operandi may be fine for those expecting a temporary posting, for anyone wanting to seriously do business in China, such an approach is not only short sighted but also actively damaging to business prospects.

If you want to find out about China, both beforehand and while you are there, by all means use the seasoned advice of experienced expatriates and also the internet and/or books to find out about the local business etiquette and culture (I have included some useful links in the section that follows). But also find out about and experience the culture itself, not through the optic of other Western expatriates but through local Chinese people. They are your greatest resource and source of information.

There is a rich seam of travel literature about China, and many books of personal experience by Western writers while trekking, searching for some lost destination, exploring off the beaten track, finding the heart of a city or living with the Chinese. Pilgrimages, odysseys, quests, confessions, discoveries: all these and more have created a fascinating tradition of Western travel writing on China.

Find books about Chinese cuisine too, about Buddhism and Islam, about history and invasions, about the Forbidden City and the Chinese imperial dynasties. Anything that adds to your understanding of the country will add a vital extra dimension to your business skills and hence to your prospects.

If you really immerse yourself, you may find — as I do — that you cannot avoid being tempted by the Chinese movie on your long-haul flight to the East, that you really want to find out what is in that strange-looking bowl of rice and chicken claws and mushroom mixed with seaweed in the local Chinese restaurant. In this case, a little knowledge is not a dangerous thing. It is essential for doing business in China.

In order to help you prepare a mental checklist and map out an initial plan of action, I have listed below a summary of the most important action points from this book:

Twelve action points — summary

1. Find out everything you can about the city or province in which you plan to operate: the principle religion or beliefs (Confucianism, Buddhism or Islam), the nuances of respect and hierarchy, the attitude to harmony and collectivism and family values, and above all the guanxi networks.

2. Research whether non-economic issues such as family ownership, local government and other loyalty structures will influence the business

models you encounter. Take advice from experienced expatriates and China consultants, as well as from locals.

3. Be aware of the importance and etiquette of business card exchange in China. Make sure all your details are on the card and that English is printed on one side and Simplified Chinese on the other. Always have an abundant stock of business cards. Practise the art of politely giving and receiving business cards with a colleague.

4. Inform yourself fully on the negotiation practices in your city or province, the incidence of corruption, and the habits of gifts or commissions that you or your representative will have to navigate.

5. Try to come to terms with the concept of face (giving, saving and losing it), which is essential in dealing with Chinese. Avoid putting possible clients and partners in 'yes-no' situations, and expect oblique answers as part of the process of creating a relationship.

6. Prepare yourself for attendance at local festivals and business dinners by learning what to give as gifts, what not to give as gifts, how to behave at banquets and home visits, and how not to give offence but to be a celebrated guest.

7. Give yourself face by presenting letters of introduction from business leaders (local or expatriate) known to your hosts, overseas members

of the local business community, and former government officials who have dealt with the country.

8. Provide precise and clear written information in both Simplified Chinese and English on your company, your proposal and what your clients have said about you for use at the initial meetings and beforehand.

9. Be ready to build up a network of guanxi relationships that will bear fruit in the long term rather than the short term. Get people on your team who have a working knowledge of the particular Chinese market and regulatory environment for your business or industry.

10. Rather than try to learn Chinese in any depth at first, pick up some simple local phrases and expressions that can be dropped into conversation as an ice-breaker: such as normal courtesies and greetings, as well as an occasional sayings that everyone will recognise.

11. In presentations or meetings, be prepared to be scrutinised and adapt your words, your timing and your body language accordingly. Learn to expect silences and pauses for your words to be digested. Always make sure to present yourself well in all senses and that your personal branding is top class.

12. Show cultural (and political) sensitivity and build up a network of business associates and a local

team that reflects the ethnic and social diversity of your city or province. Demonstrate fair-mindedness and inclusivity at all times.

Congratulations! You have reached the end of *The Master Key to China*. I hope that the points made in the book will help you as you develop your business in China and I look forward to hearing from you on your progress and how I can be of further service to you.

Remember, this is just the beginning of the journey. There is no quick recipe for success in China, because everything is built on trust and credibility and long-term relationships. Your progress may be fast or slow depending on which city or province you choose and how deeply you want to engage.

I have listed below some links to books on China that I have found especially helpful or interesting as 'master keys' to the business culture of China. I have also added links to some of my own books on China and/or Asia that I have written while being on the road as a travel writer in business class (or a businessman in coach class). They can be found in more detail at www.davidcliveprice.com/books-articles.

All these books are simply suggestive of the fascinating diversity and richness of life in China, which you as a business person will be able to explore, enjoy and harness to build long-term relationships and reap future business rewards. I hope you find them useful and I wish you the greatest success!

David Clive Price
International Cultural Expert & Revenue
Growth Strategist

www.davidcliveprice.com
www.linkedin.com/in/davidcliveprice
www.youtube.com/davidcliveprice
www.facebook.com/davidcliveprice
www.twitter.com/davidcliveprice
For questions and enquiries,
email david@davidcliveprice.com

RESOURCES AND LINKS

What's Next?
Your free 'Chinese Communication and Culture Cheat Sheet'
http://davidcliveprice.com/the-master-key-to-china-book-gift/

Ask The Master Key to China coach a question by email
david@davidcliveprice.com

Useful Links
http://www.amazon.com/Must-read-books-business-China/
lm/2P0TNBW4KG05F

http://www.amazon.co.uk/The-Economist-Doing-Business-China/dp/1846682819

http://www.newyorker.com/online/blogs/
evanosnos/2012/05/five-books-on-china.html

http://www.chinalawblog.com/2013/02/a-new-china-book-list.html

http://www.amazon.com/SAVING-FACE-CHINA-First-Hand-Traveller-ebook/dp/B005804DT2/ref=pd_sim_kstore_2

http://www.travelchinaguide.com/essential/media.htm

http://www.onlinenewspapers.com/china.htm

http://www.timeoutbeijing.com/

http://www.timeoutshanghai.com/

http://evansonmarketing.com/2013/10/13/the-top-social-media-sites-in-china-an-infographic/

http://www.amazon.com/China-Travel-Guide-Chinese-Phrase/lm/R70E10O2K28G7

http://edition.cnn.com/ASIANOW/media.sites.html#China

Selected Books

China
China's Megatrends: The 8 Pillars of a New Society by John and Doris Naisbitt, Harper Business 2010

Chinese Business Etiquette, The Practical Pocket Guide, Stefan H.Verstappen, Stone Bridge Press 2008

Harvard Business Review on Doing Business in China (Harvard Business Review Paperback Series) by Harvard Business School Press 2004

The China Dream: The Quest for the Last Great Untapped Market on Earth by Joe Studwell, Grove Press 2005

The Chinese Tao of Business: The Logic of Successful Business Strategy by George T. Haley, John Wiley & Sons (Asia) 2004

The Fragile Bridge: Conflict Management in Chinese Business, Andrew Hupert, Amazon Kindle 2012

The New Silk Road: Secrets of Business Success in China Today by John B. Stuttard, John Wiley & Sons 2000

Live & Work in China & Hong Kong, Jocelyn Kan and Hakwan Lau, Crimson Publishing 2008

On China, Henry Kissinger, Penguin Books 2012

Asia and China

Asian Business Customs and Manners, Mary Murray Bosrock, Meadowbrook Press 2007

Asian Ways, A Westerner's Guide to Asian Business Etiquette, Nick French, Aardvark Press 2008

Culture + Business in Asia, Maureen Girdham, Palgrave Macmillan 2009

Kiss, Bow, or Shake Hands Asia, Terri Morrison and Wayne A. Conway, Adams Media 2007

The Traveler's Guide to Asian Customs and Manners, Elizabeth Devine and Nancy L. Braganti, St. Martin's Griffin 1998

ABOUT THE AUTHOR

DAVID CLIVE PRICE is an author, speaker, coach and consultant on Asia's business practices and cultures. For many years he has travelled the region writing about its richly diverse peoples, traditions, beliefs and history.

In 1995, he took up the post of Executive Speechwriter for Asia for the HSBC Group in preparation for Hong Kong's reversion to Chinese sovereignty in 1997. After the 'handover', he set up his own company in Hong Kong, writing presentations and advising companies on their strategic communications in China and in Asia as a whole. His experience with many Chinese and Asia-wide multinationals gave him the idea of marrying his business experience with his knowledge of Chinese culture.

'It occurred to me that I had something unique to offer to companies entering the Chinese market or expanding in the region: not just inside knowledge of how Chinese companies operate at the highest level, but also of the business environment in which they operate. I was a travel writer in business class, or (more often) a businessman in coach class, scribbling ideas and notes for books while preparing investor presentations and attending business meetings. Why not share my knowledge and help others on the road to success?'

The result was a stream of books on Asia, including *Within the Forbidden City, Buddhism in Asia, Neon City: Hong Kong, Travels in Japan, Moonlight over Korea* and *The Master Key to Asia*. Now he has published *The Master Key to China* for those companies, SMEs and entrepreneurs that want to understand China and its cultures and traditions better as a means to optimise their business operations, maximise their revenue growth and build brand recognition in new markets.

www.davidcliveprice.com

www.linkedin.com/in/davidcliveprice

www.facebook.com/davidcliveprice

www.twitter.com/davidcliveprice

www.youtube.com

BOOKS FROM THE AUTHOR IN THE MASTER KEY SERIES™

The Master Key to Asia: A 6-Step Guide to Unlocking New Markets
The Master Key to China

CONTACT INFORMATION AND OTHER PRODUCTS AND SERVICES

If you believe your friends and colleagues would get something valuable out of this book, I'd be honoured if you post your thoughts on www.facebook.com/davidcliveprice or recommend the book on Twitter and LinkedIn.

If you feel particularly strongly about the contributions this book made to your business in China, I'd be very grateful if you posted a review on Amazon. Any points raised or questions you would like to pursue can be sent to me directly at david@davidcliveprice.com.

Finally, if you want to go further and deeper into individual markets in China or Asia, you can find further information on my International Business Passport™ keynote programmes and the Master Key Series™ at my website, www.davidcliveprice.com.

Lightning Source UK Ltd.
Milton Keynes UK
UKOW04f2339250214

227176UK00002B/83/P